WITHDRAWAL

The Twentieth-Century Novel in English: A Checklist

The Twentieth-Century Novel in English: A Checklist

By

E. C. BUFKIN

❧ ❧

UNIVERSITY OF GEORGIA PRESS

ATHENS

Preface

THE object of this book is to provide a full listing of the novels of all the major and many of the minor writers in English, regardless of nationality, who have published the entirety or the greater part of their work in the twentieth century.

The term *novel* I have used to mean, simply, any work of narrative prose fiction that was published separately in book form and was not later included, by its author, in a collection. Thus, for example, Saul Bellow's "Seize the Day" has been omitted because it first appeared in a volume with stories and a play, not separately; and Katherine Anne Porter's "Noon Wine" and James Purdy's "63: Dream Palace" have been omitted because, though originally issued as separate works, they were later incorporated in collections—the first in *Pale Horse, Pale Rider*, the second in *Color of Darkness*. Obviously, *collection* does not refer to trilogies (*The Forsyte Saga*), tetralogies (*Parade's End*), sequences (*The Music of Time*), or other omnibus volumes of novels. The exceptions to this principle are incomplete, fragmentary, and posthumous novels that have been published in volumes with other works (Evelyn Waugh's *Work Suspended*, Firbank's *The New Rythum*, Hammett's *Tulip*, Lawrence's *Mr. Noon*, Gertrude Stein's *Mrs. Reynolds*, etc.).

Novel also includes, here, the separately published, uncollected novella or novellette (such as Evelyn Waugh's *Scott-King's Modern Europe* and Eudora Welty's *The Robber Bridegroom*) and the long story (such as Firbank's *Santal* and Evelyn Waugh's *Love Among the Ruins* and *Basil Seal Rides Again*). Surely the shortest work listed is one its author stated he conceived and, despite its brevity, published as a novel—Beckett's *Imagination Dead Imagine*, which is only fourteen pages long.

Some works included in this checklist might be convincingly termed short story collections. One thinks at once of Faulkner's *Go Down, Moses.* Yet, because Faulkner himself considered this work a novel, it has been listed. Conversely, some story collections unified by character or setting, such as Maugham's *Ashenden,* Faulkner's *Knight's Gambit,* Auchincloss' *The Romantic Egoists,* and especially Anderson's *Winesburg, Ohio,* might be considered novels. These and similar works, however, are generally classified as short story collections; I have therefore not included them as novels.

I have also omitted novels written for juveniles. Some exceptions have nonetheless been made, since the works have been appropriated, as it were, by adult readers: for example, Buchan's *Prester John* and T. H. White's *Mistress Masham's Repose.*

The entries are arranged by authors in alphabetical order. The list of each writer's novels, including collaborations, is complete (through 1966), not selective; original paperbacks have been included. The title of each novel is followed by place of publication, publisher, and year. Reissues and revised editions with new titles are noted. Names in quotation marks, following the title in parentheses, indicate pseudonyms. For British authors, and most Commonwealth authors, the first English edition is given; for American authors, the first American edition. I have not, however, attempted to establish *the* first edition whenever English and American publications of the same work occurred in the *same* year: this is a matter for the specialized bibliography of an individual author. When a British novel first appeared in the United States or some other country in an *earlier* year than it appeared in England—or when an American novel first appeared in England or elsewhere before it appeared in the United States—then both editions are recorded, with dates. (The sole exceptions: the Paris and London editions of *Ulysses,* both 1922; the Florence and London editions of Lawrence's *The Virgin and the Gipsy,* both 1930.) When the same work appeared under different titles in England and the United States, both titles are given. The title by which the work is best known is listed first (thus *Prancing Nigger* before *Sorrow in Sunlight,* etc.).

The names of publishers appear in short form; in every case *Press,* when part of the name, has been omitted.

E. C. BUFKIN

Department of English
University of Georgia

The Twentieth-Century Novel in English: A Checklist

PETER [HENRY] ABRAHAMS (1919-   )
SONG OF THE CITY. London: Crisp, 1945
MINE BOY. London: Crisp, 1946
THE PATH OF THUNDER. New York: Harper, 1948. London: Faber & Faber, 1952
WILD CONQUEST. New York: Harper, 1950. London: Faber & Faber, 1951
A WREATH FOR UDOMO. London: Faber & Faber, 1956
A NIGHT OF THEIR OWN. London: Faber & Faber, 1965
THIS ISLAND NOW. London: Faber & Faber, 1966

[ALBERT] CHINUA ACHEBE (1930-   )
THINGS FALL APART. London: Heinemann, 1958
NO LONGER AT EASE. London: Heinemann, 1960
ARROW OF GOD. London: Heinemann, 1964
A MAN OF THE PEOPLE. London: Heinemann, 1966

J[OE] R[ANDOLPH] ACKERLEY (1896-   )
WE THINK THE WORLD OF YOU. London: Bodley Head, 1960. *W. H. Smith & Son Literary Award, 1962*

JAMES [RUFUS] AGEE (1909-1955)
THE MORNING WATCH. Boston: Houghton Mifflin, 1951
A DEATH IN THE FAMILY (*unfinished*). New York: McDowell, Obolensky, 1957. *Pulitzer Prize, 1958*

1

CONRAD [POTTER] AIKEN (1889-   )
BLUE VOYAGE. New York: Scribner, 1927
GREAT CIRCLE. New York: Scribner, 1933
KING COFFIN. New York: Scribner, 1935
A HEART FOR THE GODS OF MEXICO. London: Secker &
    Warburg, 1939. New York: Holt, Rinehart & Winston, 1964,
    in THE COLLECTED NOVELS OF CONRAD AIKEN
CONVERSATION. New York: Duell, Sloan & Pearce, 1940

RICHARD ALDINGTON (1892-1962)
DEATH OF A HERO. London: Chatto & Windus, 1929 (*abridged*).
    London: Consul Books, 1965 (*unabridged*)
THE COLONEL'S DAUGHTER. London: Chatto & Windus, 1931
ALL MEN ARE ENEMIES. London: Chatto & Windus, 1933
WOMEN MUST WORK. London: Chatto & Windus, 1934
VERY HEAVEN. London: Heinemann, 1937
SEVEN AGAINST REEVES. London: Heinemann, 1938
REJECTED GUEST. London: Heinemann, 1939
THE ROMANCE OF CASANOVA. New York: Duell, Sloan &
    Pearce, 1946. London: Heinemann, 1947

NELSON ALGREN (1909-   )
SOMEBODY IN BOOTS. New York: Vanguard, 1935
NEVER COME MORNING. New York: Harper, 1942
THE MAN WITH THE GOLDEN ARM. Garden City: Doubleday,
    1949. *National Book Award, 1950*
A WALK ON THE WILD SIDE. New York: Farrar, Straus &
    Cudahy, 1956

[WILLIAM] HERVEY ALLEN (1889-1949)
ANTHONY ADVERSE. New York: Farrar & Rinehart, 1933
ACTION AT AQUILA. New York: Farrar & Rinehart, 1938
THE FOREST AND THE FORT.[1] New York: Farrar & Rinehart,
    1943
BEDFORD VILLAGE.[1] New York: Farrar & Rinehart, 1944
TOWARD THE MORNING.[1] New York: Rinehart, 1948

[1]A series entitled THE DISINHERITED; collected, with a fourth, incomplete
    novel (bearing the title of the whole), as THE CITY IN THE DAWN,
    New York: Rinehart, 1950

ERIC AMBLER (1909-   )

THE DARK FRONTIER. London: Hodder & Stoughton, 1936
UNCOMMON DANGER. London: Hodder & Stoughton, 1937. New
York: Knopf, 1937, under the title BACKGROUND TO
DANGER[1,2]
EPITAPH FOR A SPY. London: Hodder & Stoughton, 1938
CAUSE FOR ALARM.[1,2] London: Hodder & Stoughton, 1938
THE MASK OF DIMITRIOS.[4] London: Hodder & Stoughton, 1939.
New York: Knopf, 1939, under the title A COFFIN FOR
DIMITRIOS[2]
JOURNEY INTO FEAR.[2,4] London: Hodder & Stoughton, 1940
SKYTIP (in collaboration with Charles Rodda; by "Eliot Reed").
Garden City: Doubleday, 1950. London: Hodder & Stoughton,
1951
TENDER TO MOONLIGHT (in collaboration with Charles Rodda;
by "Eliot Reed"). London: Hodder & Stoughton, 1952. Garden
City: Doubleday, 1951, under the title TENDER TO DANGER
JUDGMENT ON DELTCHEV.[3,4] London: Hodder & Stoughton,
1951
THE MARAS AFFAIR (in collaboration with Charles Rodda; by
"Eliot Reed"). Garden City: Doubleday, 1953. London: Collins,
1955
THE SCHIRMER INHERITANCE.[3] London: Heinemann, 1953
CHARTER TO DANGER (in collaboration with Charles Rodda;
by "Eliot Reed"). London: Collins, 1954
THE NIGHT-COMERS. London: Heinemann, 1956. New York:
Knopf, 1956, under the title STATE OF SIEGE[3]
PASSPORT TO PANIC (in collaboration with Charles Rodda; by
"Eliot Reed"). London: Collins, 1958
PASSAGE OF ARMS.[3] London: Heinemann, 1959
THE LIGHT OF DAY. London: Heinemann, 1962
A KIND OF ANGER. London: Bodley Head, 1964
[1]Collected as DOUBLE DECKER, Cleveland: World, 1945
[2]Collected as INTRIGUE, New York: Knopf, 1943
[3]Collected as THE INTRIGUERS, New York: Knopf, 1965
[4]Collected as INTRIGUE, London: Holder & Stoughton, 1965

KINGSLEY [WILLIAM] AMIS (1922-   )

LUCKY JIM. London: Gollancz, 1954. *Somerset Maugham Award,
1955*
THAT UNCERTAIN FEELING. London: Gollancz, 1955
I LIKE IT HERE. London: Gollancz, 1958
TAKE A GIRL LIKE YOU. London: Gollancz, 1960

ONE FAT ENGLISHMAN. London: Gollancz, 1963
THE EGYPTOLOGISTS (in collaboration with Robert Conquest).
London: Cape, 1965
THE ANTI-DEATH LEAGUE. London: Gollancz, 1966

MULK RAJ ANAND (1905-)
UNTOUCHABLE. London: Wishart, 1935
THE COOLIE. London: Lawrence & Wishart, 1936. Reissued as
COOLIE, Harmondsworth, Middlesex: Penguin Books, 1945
TWO LEAVES AND A BUD. London: Lawrence & Wishart, 1937
THE VILLAGE.[1] London: Cape, 1939
ACROSS THE BLACK WATERS.[1] London: Cape, 1940
THE SWORD AND THE SICKLE.[1] London: Cape, 1942
THE BIG HEART. London: Hutchinson, 1945
SEVEN SUMMERS. London: Hutchinson, 1951
PRIVATE LIFE OF AN INDIAN PRINCE. London: Hutchinson,
1953
THE OLD WOMAN AND THE COW. Bombay: Kutub-Popular,
1960
THE ROAD. Bombay: Kutub-Popular, 1961
DEATH OF A HERO. Bombay: Kutub-Popular, 1963
[1]A trilogy

SHERWOOD ANDERSON (1876-1941)
WINDY McPHERSON'S SON. New York: Lane, 1916
MARCHING MEN. New York: Lane, 1917
POOR WHITE. New York: Huebsch, 1920
MANY MARRIAGES. New York: Huebsch, 1923
DARK LAUGHTER. New York: Boni & Liveright, 1925
TAR. New York: Boni & Liveright, 1926
BEYOND DESIRE. New York: Liveright, 1932
KIT BRANDON. New York: Scribner, 1936

CICILY ISABEL FAIRFIELD ANDREWS:
See REBECCA WEST

CORINNE ANDREWS: See REBECCA WEST

PIERRE ANDRÉZEL: See ISAK DINESEN

WINIFRED ASHTON: See CLEMENCE DANE

SYLVIA ASHTON-WARNER (-   )
SPINSTER. London: Secker & Warburg, 1958
INCENSE TO IDOLS. London: Secker & Warburg, 1960
BELL CALL. New York: Simon & Schuster, 1965
GREENSTONE. New York: Simon & Schuster, 1966

JAMES ASTON: See T[ERENCE] H[ANBURY] WHITE

LOUIS [STANTON] AUCHINCLOSS (1917-   )
THE INDIFFERENT CHILDREN (by "Andrew Lee"). New York: Prentice-Hall, 1947
SYBIL. Boston: Houghton Mifflin, 1952
A LAW FOR THE LION. Boston: Houghton Mifflin, 1953
THE GREAT WORLD AND TIMOTHY COLT. Boston: Houghton Mifflin, 1956
VENUS IN SPARTA. Boston: Houghton Mifflin, 1958
PURSUIT OF THE PRODIGAL. Boston: Houghton Mifflin, 1959
THE HOUSE OF FIVE TALENTS. Boston: Houghton Mifflin, 1960
PORTRAIT IN BROWNSTONE. Boston: Houghton Mifflin, 1962
THE RECTOR OF JUSTIN. Boston: Houghton Mifflin, 1964
THE EMBEZZLER. Boston: Houghton Mifflin, 1966

MARY [HUNTER] AUSTIN (1868-1934)
ISIDRO. Boston: Houghton Mifflin, 1905
SANTA LUCIA. New York: Harper, 1908
OUTLAND (in collaboration with George Sterling; by "George Stairs"). London: Murray, 1910. New York: Boni & Liveright, 1919 (by Mary Austin)
A WOMAN OF GENIUS. Garden City: Doubleday, Page, 1912
THE GREEN BOUGH. Garden City: Doubleday, Page, 1913
THE LOVELY LADY. Garden City: Doubleday, Page, 1913
THE FORD. Boston: Houghton Mifflin, 1917
NO. 26 JAYNE STREET. Boston: Houghton Mifflin, 1920
STARRY ADVENTURE. Boston: Houghton Mifflin, 1931

NIGEL [MARLIN] BALCHIN (1908-   )
NO SKY. London: Hamilton, 1934
SIMPLE LIFE. London: Hamilton, 1935
LIGHTBODY ON LIBERTY. London: Collins, 1936
DARKNESS FALLS FROM THE AIR. London: Collins, 1942

THE SMALL BACK ROOM. London: Collins, 1943
MINE OWN EXECUTIONER. London: Collins, 1945
LORD, I WAS AFRAID. London: Collins, 1947
THE BORGIA TESTAMENT. London: Collins, 1948
A SORT OF TRAITORS. London: Collins, 1949. Boston: Houghton
    Mifflin, 1949, under the title WHO IS MY NEIGHBOR?
A WAY THROUGH THE WOOD. London: Collins, 1951
SUNDRY CREDITORS. London: Collins, 1953. Boston: Houghton
    Mifflin, 1953,·under the title PRIVATE INTERESTS
THE FALL OF THE SPARROW. London: Collins, 1955. New
    York: Rinehart, 1956, under the title THE FALL OF A
    SPARROW
SEEN DIMLY BEFORE DAWN. London: Collins, 1962
IN THE ABSENCE OF MRS. PETERSEN. London: Collins, 1966

JAMES [ARTHUR] BALDWIN (1924-   )

GO TELL IT ON THE MOUNTAIN. New York: Knopf, 1953
GIOVANNI'S ROOM. New York: Dial, 1956
ANOTHER COUNTRY. New York: Dial, 1962

DJUNA BARNES (1892-   )

RYDER. New York: Liveright, 1928
NIGHTWOOD. London: Faber & Faber, 1936. New York: Har-
    court, Brace, 1937

ALAN GABRIEL BARNSLEY: See GABRIEL FIELDING

JOHN [SIMMONS] BARTH (1930-   )

THE FLOATING OPERA. New York: Appleton-Century-Crofts,
    1956
THE END OF THE ROAD. Garden City: Doubleday, 1958
THE SOT-WEED FACTOR. Garden City: Doubleday, 1960
GILES GOAT-BOY. Garden City: Doubleday, 1966

[JOSEPH] HAMILTON BASSO (1904-1964)

RELICS AND ANGELS. New York: Macaulay, 1929
CINNAMON SEED. New York: Scribner, 1934
IN THEIR OWN IMAGE. New York: Scribner, 1935
COURT-HOUSE SQUARE. New York: Scribner, 1936
DAYS BEFORE LENT. New York: Scribner, 1939

WINE OF THE COUNTRY. New York: Scribner, 1941
SUN IN CAPRICORN. New York: Scribner, 1942
THE GREENROOM. Garden City: Doubleday, 1949
THE VIEW FROM POMPEY'S HEAD. Garden City: Doubleday,
    1954. London: Collins, 1955, under the title POMPEY'S HEAD
THE LIGHT INFANTRY BALL. Garden City: Doubleday, 1959
A TOUCH OF THE DRAGON. New York: Viking, 1964

H[ERBERT] E[RNEST] BATES (1905-)

THE TWO SISTERS. London: Cape, 1926
CATHERINE FOSTER. London: Cape, 1929
CHARLOTTE'S ROW. London: Cape, 1931
THE FALLOW LAND. London: Cape, 1932
THE POACHER. London: Cape, 1935
A HOUSE OF WOMEN. London: Cape, 1936
SPELLA HO. London: Cape, 1938
FAIR STOOD THE WIND FOR FRANCE. London: Joseph, 1944
THE CRUISE OF THE BREADWINNER. London: Joseph, 1946
THE PURPLE PLAIN. London: Joseph, 1947
THE JACARANDA TREE. London: Joseph, 1949
DEAR LIFE. Boston: Atlantic-Little, Brown, 1949; London:
    Joseph, 1950
THE SCARLET SWORD. London: Joseph, 1950
LOVE FOR LYDIA. London: Joseph, 1952
THE FEAST OF JULY. London: Joseph, 1954
THE SLEEPLESS MOON. London: Joseph, 1956
THE DARLING BUDS OF MAY. London: Joseph, 1958
A BREATH OF FRENCH AIR. London: Joseph, 1959
WHEN THE GREEN WOODS LAUGH. London: Joseph, 1960.
    Boston: Atlantic-Little, Brown, 1961, under the title HARK,
    HARK, THE LARK!
THE DAY OF THE TORTOISE. London: Joseph, 1961
A CROWN OF WILD MYRTLE. London: Joseph, 1962
OH, TO BE IN ENGLAND! London: Joseph, 1963
A MOMENT IN TIME. London: Joseph, 1964

RALPH BATES (1899-)

LEAN MEN. London: Davies, 1934
THE OLIVE FIELD. London: Cape, 1936
THE FIELDS OF PARADISE. New York: Dutton, 1940. London:
    Cape, 1941
THE DOLPHIN IN THE WOOD. London: Hart-Davis, 1950

SAMUEL [BARCLAY] BECKETT (1906-   )
MURPHY. London: Routledge, 1938
WATT. Paris: Olympia, 1953. London: Zwemmer, 1958
MOLLOY.[1,2] New York: Grove, 1955
MALONE DIES.[1,2] New York: Grove, 1956. London: Calder, 1958
THE UNNAMABLE.[1,2] New York: Grove, 1958
HOW IT IS.[1] London: Calder, 1964. *Prix International de Littérature, 1961 [French version]*
IMAGINATION DEAD IMAGINE.[1] London: Calder & Boyars, 1966
[1]Originally written in French
[2]A trilogy: New York: Grove, 1959; London: Calder, 1960

SYBILLE BEDFORD (1911-   )
A LEGACY. London: Weidenfeld & Nicolson, 1956
A FAVOURITE OF THE GODS. London: Collins, 1963

Sir MAX BEERBOHM (1872-1956)
ZULEIKA DOBSON. London: Heinemann, 1911

BRENDAN [FRANCIS] BEHAN (1923-1964)
THE SCARPERER. Garden City: Doubleday, 1964. London: Hutchinson, 1966

SAUL BELLOW (1915-   )
DANGLING MAN. New York: Vanguard, 1944
THE VICTIM. New York: Vanguard, 1947
THE ADVENTURES OF AUGIE MARCH. New York: Viking, 1953. *National Book Award, 1954*
HENDERSON THE RAIN KING. New York: Viking, 1959
HERZOG. New York: Viking, 1964. *National Book Award, 1965. Prix International de Littérature, 1965*

[ENOCH] ARNOLD BENNETT (1867-1931)
A MAN FROM THE NORTH. London: Lane, 1898
THE GRAND BABYLON HOTEL. London: Chatto & Windus, 1902. New York: New Amsterdam, 1902, under the title T. RACKSOLE AND DAUGHTER
ANNA OF THE FIVE TOWNS. London: Chatto & Windus, 1902
THE GATES OF WRATH. London: Chatto & Windus, 1903
LEONORA. London: Chatto & Windus, 1903
A GREAT MAN. London: Chatto & Windus, 1904

TERESA OF WATLING STREET. London: Chatto & Windus, 1904

THE LOOT OF CITIES. London: Rivers, 1905

SACRED AND PROFANE LOVE. London: Chatto & Windus, 1905. New York: Doran, 1911, under the title THE BOOK OF CARLOTTA

HUGO. London: Chatto & Windus, 1906

WHOM GOD HATH JOINED. London: Nutt, 1906

THE SINEWS OF WAR (in collaboration with Eden Phillpotts). London: Laurie, 1906. New York: McClure, Phillips, 1906, under the title DOUBLOONS

THE GHOST. London: Chatto & Windus, 1907

THE CITY OF PLEASURE. London: Chatto & Windus, 1907

THE STATUE (in collaboration with Eden Phillpotts). London: Cassell, 1908

BURIED ALIVE. London: Chapman & Hall, 1908

THE OLD WIVES' TALE. London: Chapman & Hall, 1908

THE GLIMPSE. London: Chapman & Hall, 1909

HELEN WITH THE HIGH HAND. London: Chapman & Hall, 1910

CLAYHANGER.[1] London: Methuen, 1910

THE CARD. London: Methuen, 1911. New York: Dutton, 1911, under the title DENRY THE AUDACIOUS

HILDA LESSWAYS.[1] London: Methuen, 1911

THE REGENT. London: Methuen, 1913. New York: Doran, 1913, under the title THE OLD ADAM

THE PRICE OF LOVE. London: Methuen, 1914

THESE TWAIN.[1] New York: Doran, 1915. London: Methuen, 1916

THE LION'S SHARE. London: Cassell, 1916

THE PRETTY LADY. London: Cassell, 1918

THE ROLL-CALL. London: Hutchinson, 1918

MR. PROHACK. London: Methuen, 1922

LILIAN. London: Cassell, 1922

RICEYMAN STEPS. London: Cassell, 1923. *James Tait Black Memorial Prize, 1924*

LORD RINGO. London: Cassell, 1926

THE STRANGE VANGUARD. London: Cassell, 1928. New York: Doran, 1927, under the title THE VANGUARD

ACCIDENT. Garden City: Doubleday, Doran, 1928. London: Cassell, 1929

PICCADILLY. London: Readers' Library, 1929

IMPERIAL PALACE. London: Cassell, 1930

VENUS RISING FROM THE SEA. London: Cassell, 1931. Garden

City: Doubleday, Doran, 1932, under the title STROKE OF
   LUCK
DREAM OF DESTINY (*unfinished*). London: Cassell, 1932
[1]A trilogy: THE CLAYHANGER FAMILY, London: Methuen, 1925

STELLA BENSON (1892-1933)
I POSE. London: Macmillan, 1915
THIS IS THE END. London: Macmillan, 1917
LIVING ALONE. London: Macmillan, 1919
THE POOR MAN. London: Macmillan, 1922
PIPERS AND A DANCER. London: Macmillan, 1924
GOODBYE, STRANGER. London: Macmillan, 1926
TOBIT TRANSPLANTED. London: Macmillan, 1931. New York:
   Harper, 1930, under the title THE FAR-AWAY BRIDE.
   Femina-Vie Heureuse Prize, 1932
MUNDOS (*unfinished*). London: Macmillan, 1935

PHYLLIS [ELEANOR] BENTLEY (1894-   )
ENVIRONMENT. London: Sidgwick & Jackson, 1922
CAT-IN-THE-MANGER. London: Sidgwick & Jackson, 1923
THE SPINNER OF THE YEARS. London: Benn, 1928
THE PARTNERSHIP. London: Benn, 1928
CARR. London: Benn, 1929
TRIO. London: Gollancz, 1930
INHERITANCE.[1] London: Gollancz, 1932
A MODERN TRAGEDY. London: Gollancz, 1934
FREEDOM, FAREWELL! London: Gollancz, 1936
SLEEP IN PEACE. London: Gollancz, 1938
TAKE COURAGE. London: Gollancz, 1940. New York: Macmillan,
   1940, under the title THE POWER AND THE GLORY
MANHOLD. London: Gollancz, 1941
THE RISE OF HENRY MORCAR.[1] London: Gollancz, 1946
LIFE STORY. London: Gollancz, 1948
QUORUM. London: Gollancz, 1950
THE HOUSE OF MOREYS. London: Gollancz, 1953
NOBLE IN REASON. London: Gollancz, 1955
CRESCENDO. London: Gollancz, 1958
A MAN OF HIS TIME.[1] London: Gollancz, 1966
[1]A trilogy

J[OHN] D[AVYS] BERESFORD (1873-1947)
THE EARLY HISTORY OF JACOB STAHL.[1] London: Sidgwick &
   Jackson, 1911

THE HAMPDENSHIRE WONDER. London: Sidgwick & Jackson, 1911. New York: Doran, 1917, under the title THE WONDER
A CANDIDATE FOR TRUTH.[1] London: Sidgwick & Jackson, 1912
GOSLINGS. London: Heinemann, 1913. New York: Macaulay, 1913, under the title A WORLD OF WOMEN
THE HOUSE IN DEMETRIUS ROAD. London: Heinemann, 1914
THE INVISIBLE EVENT.[1] London: Sidgwick & Jackson, 1915
THE MOUNTAINS OF THE MOON. London: Cassell, 1915
THESE LYNNEKERS. London: Cassell, 1916
HOUSE-MATES. London: Cassell, 1917
GOD'S COUNTERPOINT. London: Collins, 1918
THE JERVAISE COMEDY. London: Collins, 1919
AN IMPERFECT MOTHER. London: Collins, 1920
REVOLUTION. London: Collins, 1921
THE PRISONERS OF HARTLING. London: Collins, 1922
LOVE'S PILGRIM. London: Collins, 1923
UNITY. London: Collins, 1924
THE MONKEY-PUZZLE. London: Collins, 1925
THAT KIND OF MAN. London: Collins, 1926. Indianapolis: Bobbs-Merrill, 1926, under the title ALMOST PAGAN
THE TAPESTRY. London: Collins, 1927
THE DECOY. London: Collins, 1927
ALL OR NOTHING. London: Collins, 1928
THE INSTRUMENT OF DESTINY. London: Collins, 1928
REAL PEOPLE. London: Collins, 1929
LOVE'S ILLUSION. London: Collins, 1930
SEVEN, BOBSWORTH. London: Faber & Faber, 1930
AN INNOCENT CRIMINAL. London: Collins, 1931
THE OLD PEOPLE.[2] London: Collins, 1931
THE NEXT GENERATION. London: Benn, 1932
THE MIDDLE GENERATION.[2] London: Collins, 1932
THE YOUNG PEOPLE.[2] London: Collins, 1933
THE INHERITOR. London: Benn, 1933
THE CAMBERWELL MIRACLE. London: Heinemann, 1933
PECKOVER. London: Heinemann, 1934
ON A HUGE HILL. London: Heinemann, 1935
THE FAITHFUL LOVERS. London: Hutchinson, 1936
CLEO. London: Hutchinson, 1937
THE UNFINISHED ROAD. London: Hutchinson, 1938
SNELL'S FOLLY. London: Hutchinson, 1939
STRANGE RIVAL. London: Hutchinson, 1939
QUIET CORNER. London: Hutchinson, 1940
"WHAT DREAMS MAY COME . . ." London: Hutchinson, 1941

A COMMON ENEMY. London: Hutchinson, 1942
THE LONG VIEW. London: Hutchinson, 1943
MEN IN THE SAME BOAT (in collaboration with Esmé Wynne
    Tyson). London: Hutchinson, 1943
THE BENEFACTOR. London: Hutchinson, 1943
IF THIS WERE TRUE . . . London: Hutchinson, 1944
THE RIDDLE OF THE TOWER (in collaboration with Esmé
    Wynne-Tyson). London: Hutchinson, 1944
THE PRISONER. London: Hutchinson, 1946
THE GIFT (in collaboration with Esmé Wynne-Tyson). London:
    Hutchinson, 1947

[1]The Jacob Stahl trilogy
[2]A trilogy: THREE GENERATIONS

THOMAS [LOUIS] BERGER (1924-   )
CRAZY IN BERLIN. New York: Scribner, 1958
REINHART IN LOVE. New York: Scribner, 1962
LITTLE BIG MAN. New York: Dial, 1964. *Rosenthal Award, 1965*

ERIC ARTHUR BLAIR: See GEORGE ORWELL

KAREN BLIXEN: See ISAK DINESEN

VANCE [NYE] BOURJAILY (1922-   )
THE END OF MY LIFE. New York: Scribner, 1947
THE HOUND OF EARTH. New York: Scribner, 1955
THE VIOLATED. New York: Dial, 1958
CONFESSIONS OF A SPENT YOUTH. New York: Dial, 1960

ELIZABETH [DOROTHEA COLE] BOWEN, C. Litt. (1899-   )
THE HOTEL. London: Constable, 1927
THE LAST SEPTEMBER. London: Constable, 1929
FRIENDS AND RELATIONS. London: Constable, 1931
TO THE NORTH. London: Gollancz, 1932
THE HOUSE IN PARIS. London: Gollancz, 1935
THE DEATH OF THE HEART. London: Gollancz, 1938
THE HEAT OF THE DAY. London: Cape, 1949
A WORLD OF LOVE. London: Cape, 1955
THE LITTLE GIRLS. London: Cape, 1964

JOHN [GRIFFITH] BOWEN (1924-   )
THE TRUTH WILL NOT HELP US. London: Chatto & Windus, 1956
AFTER THE RAIN. London: Faber & Faber, 1958
THE CENTRE OF THE GREEN. London: Faber & Faber, 1959
STORYBOARD. London: Faber & Faber, 1960
THE BIRDCAGE. London: Faber & Faber, 1962
A WORLD ELSEWHERE. London: Faber & Faber, 1965

PAUL [FREDERIC] BOWLES (1910-   )
THE SHELTERING SKY. New York: New Directions, 1949
LET IT COME DOWN. New York: Random House, 1952
THE SPIDER'S HOUSE. New York: Random House, 1955
ABOVE THE WORLD. New York: Simon & Schuster, 1966

EDGAR BOX: See GORE VIDAL

JAMES BOYD (1888-1944)
DRUMS. New York: Scribner, 1925
MARCHING ON. New York: Scribner, 1927
LONG HUNT. New York: Scribner, 1930
ROLL RIVER. New York: Scribner, 1935
BITTER CREEK. New York: Scribner, 1939

KAY BOYLE (1903-   )
PLAGUED BY THE NIGHTINGALE. New York: Cape & Smith, 1931
YEAR BEFORE LAST. New York: Smith, 1932
GENTLEMEN, I ADDRESS YOU PRIVATELY. New York: Smith & Haas, 1933
MY NEXT BRIDE. New York: Harcourt, Brace, 1934
DEATH OF A MAN. New York: Harcourt, Brace, 1936
MONDAY NIGHT. New York: Harcourt, Brace, 1938
PRIMER FOR COMBAT. New York: Simon & Schuster, 1942
AVALANCHE. New York: Simon & Schuster, 1944
A FRENCHMAN MUST DIE. New York: Simon & Schuster, 1946
1939. New York: Simon & Schuster, 1948
HIS HUMAN MAJESTY. New York: Whittlesey House, 1949
THE SEAGULL ON THE STEP. New York: Knopf, 1955
GENERATION WITHOUT FAREWELL. New York: Knopf, 1960

GERALD WARNER BRACE (1901-   )

THE ISLANDS. New York: Putnam, 1936
THE WAYWARD PILGRIMS. New York: Putnam, 1938
LIGHT ON A MOUNTAIN. New York: Putnam, 1941
THE GARRETSON CHRONICLE. New York: Norton, 1947
A SUMMER'S TALE. New York: Norton, 1949
THE SPIRE. New York: Norton, 1952
BELL'S LANDING. New York: Norton, 1955
THE WORLD OF CARRICK'S COVE. New York: Norton, 1957
WINTER SOLSTICE. New York: Norton, 1960
THE WIND'S WILL. New York: Norton, 1964

JOHN [GERARD] BRAINE (1922-   )

ROOM AT THE TOP. London: Eyre & Spottiswoode, 1957
THE VODI. London: Eyre & Spottiswoode, 1959. Boston: Houghton
    Mifflin, 1960, under the title FROM THE HAND OF THE
    HUNTER
LIFE AT THE TOP. London: Eyre & Spottiswoode, 1962
THE JEALOUS GOD. London: Eyre & Spottiswoode, 1964

LOUIS [BRUCKER] BROMFIELD (1896-1956)

THE GREEN BAY TREE.[1] New York: Stokes, 1924
POSSESSION.[1] New York: Stokes, 1925. London: Unwin, 1926,
    under the title LILLI BARR
EARLY AUTUMN.[1] New York: Stokes, 1926. *Pulitzer Prize, 1927*
A GOOD WOMAN.[1] New York: Stokes, 1927
THE STRANGE CASE OF MISS ANNIE SPRAGG. New York:
    Stokes, 1928
TWENTY-FOUR HOURS. New York: Stokes, 1930
A MODERN HERO. New York: Stokes, 1932
THE FARM. New York: Harper, 1933
THE MAN WHO HAD EVERYTHING. New York: Harper, 1935
THE RAINS CAME. New York: Harper, 1937
NIGHT IN BOMBAY. New York: Harper, 1940
WILD IS THE RIVER. New York: Harper, 1941
UNTIL THE DAY BREAK. New York: Harper, 1942
MRS. PARKINGTON. New York: Harper, 1943
WHAT BECAME OF ANNA BOLTON. New York: Harper, 1944
COLORADO. New York: Harper, 1947
THE WILD COUNTRY. New York: Harper, 1948
MR. SMITH. New York: Harper, 1951

[1]A tetralogy: ESCAPE

CHRISTINE BROOKE-ROSE (1923-   )
THE LANGUAGES OF LOVE. London: Secker & Warburg, 1957
THE SYCAMORE TREE. London: Secker & Warburg, 1958
THE DEAR DECEIT. London: Secker & Warburg, 1960
THE MIDDLEMEN. London: Secker & Warburg, 1961
OUT. London: Joseph, 1964
SUCH. London: Joseph, 1966. *James Tait Black Memorial Prize,*
1967

BRIGID [ANTONIA] BROPHY (1929-   )
HACKENFELLER'S APE. London: Hart-Davis, 1953
THE KING OF A RAINY COUNTRY. London: Secker & Warburg,
1956
FLESH. London: Secker & Warburg, 1962
THE FINISHING TOUCH. London: Secker & Warburg, 1963
THE SNOW BALL. London: Secker & Warburg, 1964

BRYHER, i.e. [ANNIE] WINIFRED ELLERMAN (1894-   )
DEVELOPMENT. London: Constable, 1920
THE FOURTEENTH OF OCTOBER. New York: Pantheon, 1952.
London: Collins, 1954
THE PLAYER'S BOY. New York: Pantheon, 1953. London: Collins,
1957
ROMAN WALL. New York: Pantheon, 1954. London: Collins, 1955
BEOWULF.[1] New York: Pantheon, 1956
GATE TO THE SEA. New York: Pantheon, 1958. London: Collins,
1959
RUAN. New York: Pantheon, 1960. London: Collins, 1961
THE COIN OF CARTHAGE. New York: Harcourt, Brace & World,
1963. London: Collins, 1964
VISA FOR AVALON. New York: Harcourt, Brace & World, 1965
THIS JANUARY TALE. New York: Harcourt, Brace & World, 1966
[1]First published in translation in 1948, Paris: Mercure de France

JOHN BUCHAN, Lord TWEEDSMUIR (1875-1940)
SIR QUIXOTE OF THE MOORS. London: Unwin, 1895
JOHN BURNET OF BARNS. London: Lane, 1898
A LOST LADY OF OLD YEARS. London: Lane, 1899
THE HALF-HEARTED. London: Isbister, 1900

A LODGE IN THE WILDERNESS. Edinburgh: Blackwood, 1906
PRESTER JOHN. London: Nelson, 1910. New York: Dodd, Mead,
1910, under the title THE GREAT DIAMOND PIPE
THE THIRTY-NINE STEPS.[1,2] Edinburgh: Blackwood, 1915
SALUTE TO ADVENTURERS.[3] London: Nelson, 1915
THE POWER-HOUSE.[4] Edinburgh: Blackwood, 1916
GREENMANTLE.[1,2] London: Hodder & Stoughton, 1916
MR. STANDFAST.[1,2] London: Hodder & Stoughton, 1918
THE PATH OF THE KING. London: Hodder & Stoughton, 1921
HUNTINGTOWER.[5,6] London: Hodder & Stoughton, 1922
MIDWINTER.[3] London: Hodder & Stoughton, 1923
THE THREE HOSTAGES.[1,6] London: Hodder & Stoughton, 1924
JOHN MACNAB.[4,6] London: Hodder & Stoughton, 1925
THE DANCING FLOOR.[4] London: Hodder & Stoughton, 1926
WITCH WOOD.[3] London: Hodder & Stoughton, 1927
THE COURTS OF THE MORNING. London: Hodder & Stoughton,
1929
CASTLE GAY.[5] London: Hodder & Stoughton, 1930
THE BLANKET OF THE DARK.[3] London: Hodder & Stoughton,
1931
THE GAP IN THE CURTAIN.[4] London: Hodder & Stoughton, 1932
A PRINCE OF THE CAPTIVITY. London: Hodder & Stoughton,
1933
THE FREE FISHERS.[3] London: Hodder & Stoughton, 1934
THE HOUSE OF THE FOUR WINDS.[5] London: Hodder & Stough-
ton, 1935
THE ISLAND OF SHEEP. London: Hodder & Stoughton, 1936.
Boston: Houghton Mifflin, 1936, under the title THE MAN
FROM THE NORLANDS
SICK HEART RIVER. London: Hodder & Stoughton, 1941. Boston:
Houghton Mifflin, 1941, under the title MOUNTAIN MEADOW

[1]Collected as THE FOUR ADVENTURES OF RICHARD HANNAY, London:
Hodder & Stoughton, 1930
[2]Collected as ADVENTURES OF RICHARD HANNAY, Boston: Houghton
Mifflin, 1939
[3]Collected as FIVE FOLD SALUTE TO ADVENTURE, London: Hodder &
Stoughton, 1939
[4]Collected as THE ADVENTURES OF SIR EDWARD LEITHEN, London:
Hodder & Stoughton, 1935
[5]Collected as THE ADVENTURES OF DICKSON McCUNN, London: Hodder
& Stoughton, 1937
[6]Collected as ADVENTURERS ALL, Boston: Houghton Mifflin, 1942

PEARL S[YDENSTRICKER] BUCK (1892-   )

Howells Medal, American Academy of Arts and Letters, 1935.
Nobel Prize for Literature, 1938

EAST WIND: WEST WIND. New York: Day, 1930
THE GOOD EARTH.[1] New York: Day, 1931. *Pulitzer Prize, 1932.*
    Howells Medal, 1935
THE YOUNG REVOLUTIONIST. New York: Friendship, 1932
SONS.[1] New York: Day, 1932
THE MOTHER. New York: Day, 1934
A HOUSE DIVIDED.[1] New York: Reynal & Hitchcock, 1935
THIS PROUD HEART. New York: Reynal & Hitchcock, 1938
THE PATRIOT. New York: Day, 1939
OTHER GODS. New York: Day, 1940
CHINA SKY. New York: Triangle Books, 1942
DRAGON SEED. New York: Day, 1942
THE PROMISE. New York: Day, 1943
CHINA FLIGHT. Philadelphia: Blakiston, 1945
PORTRAIT OF A MARRIAGE. New York: Day, 1945
THE TOWNSMAN.[2] (by "John Sedges"). New York: Day, 1945
PAVILION OF WOMEN. New York: Day, 1946
THE ANGRY WIFE (by "John Sedges"). New York: Day, 1947
PEONY. New York: Day, 1948. London: Methuen, 1949, under
    the title THE BONDMAID
KINFOLK. New York: Day, 1949
THE LONG LOVE[2] (by "John Sedges"). New York: Day, 1949
GOD'S MEN. New York: Day, 1951
THE HIDDEN FLOWER. New York: Day, 1952
BRIGHT PROCESSION (by "John Sedges"). New York: Day, 1952
VOICES IN THE HOUSE[2] (by "John Sedges"). New York: Day,
    1953
COME, MY BELOVED. New York: Day, 1953
IMPERIAL WOMAN. New York: Day, 1956
LETTER FROM PEKING. New York: Day, 1957
COMMAND THE MORNING. New York: Day, 1959
SATAN NEVER SLEEPS. New York: Pocket Books, 1962
THE LIVING REED. New York: Day, 1963
DEATH IN THE CASTLE. New York: Day, 1965
[1]A trilogy: HOUSE OF EARTH, New York: Reynal & Hitchcock, 1935
[2]Collected as AMERICAN TRIPTYCH, New York: Day, 1958

[CARL] FREDERICK BUECHNER (1926-   )
A LONG DAY'S DYING. New York: Knopf, 1950
THE SEASONS' DIFFERENCE. New York: Knopf, 1952
THE RETURN OF ANSEL GIBBS. New York: Knopf, 1958.
    Rosenthal Award, 1959
THE FINAL BEAST. New York: Atheneum, 1965

[JOHN] ANTHONY BURGESS [WILSON] (1917-   )

TIME FOR A TIGER.[1] London: Heinemann, 1956
THE ENEMY IN THE BLANKET.[1] London: Heinemann, 1958
BEDS IN THE EAST.[1] London: Heinemann, 1959
THE RIGHT TO AN ANSWER. London: Heinemann, 1960
THE DOCTOR IS SICK. London: Heinemann, 1960
THE WORM AND THE RING. London: Heinemann, 1961
ONE HAND CLAPPING (by "Joseph Kell"). London: Davies, 1961
DEVIL OF A STATE. London: Heinemann, 1961
A CLOCKWORK ORANGE. London: Heinemann, 1962
THE WANTING SEED. London: Heinemann, 1962
HONEY FOR THE BEARS. London: Heinemann, 1963
INSIDE MR. ENDERBY (by "Joseph Kell"). London: Heinemann, 1963
NOTHING LIKE THE SUN. London: Heinemann. 1964
THE EVE OF ST. VENUS. London: Sidgwick & Jackson, 1964
A VISION OF BATTLEMENTS. London: Sidgwick & Jackson, 1965
TREMOR OF INTENT. London: Heinemann, 1966

[1]MALAYAN TRILOGY, London: Pan Books, 1964; under the title THE LONG DAY WANES, New York: Norton, 1965

LEDA BURKE: See DAVID GARNETT

JOHN HORNE BURNS (1916-1953)

THE GALLERY. New York: Harper, 1947
LUCIFER WITH A BOOK. New York: Harper, 1949
A CRY OF CHILDREN. New York: Harper, 1952

WILLIAM S[EWARD] BURROUGHS (1914-   )

THE NAKED LUNCH. Paris: Olympia, 1959. New York: Grove, 1962, under the title NAKED LUNCH
THE SOFT MACHINE. Paris: Olympia, 1961. New York: Grove, 1966
THE TICKET THAT EXPLODED. Paris: Olympia, 1962
DEAD FINGERS TALK. London: Calder, 1963
NOVA EXPRESS. New York: Grove, 1964

JAMES BRANCH CABELL (1879-1958)

THE EAGLE'S SHADOW.[1] New York: Doubleday, Page, 1904
THE CORDS OF VANITY.[1] New York: Doubleday, Page, 1909

THE SOUL OF MELICENT.[1] New York: Stokes, 1913. Reissued as DOMNEI, New York: McBride, 1920
THE RIVET IN GRANDFATHER'S NECK.[1] New York: McBride, 1915
THE CREAM OF THE JEST.[1] New York: McBride, 1917
JURGEN.[1] New York: McBride, 1919
FIGURES OF EARTH.[1] New York: McBride, 1921
THE HIGH PLACE.[1] New York: McBride, 1923
THE SILVER STALLION.[1] New York: McBride, 1926
THE MUSIC FROM BEHIND THE MOON.[1,2] New York: Day, 1926
SOMETHING ABOUT EVE.[1] New York: McBride, 1927
THE WHITE ROBE.[1,2] New York: McBride, 1928
THE WAY OF ECBEN.[1,2] New York: McBride, 1929
SMIRT[3] (by "Branch Cabell"). New York: McBride, 1934
SMITH[3] (by "Branch Cabell"). New York: McBride, 1935
SMIRE[3] (by "Branch Cabell"). Garden City: Doubleday, Doran, 1937
THE KING WAS IN HIS COUNTING HOUSE[4] (by "Branch Cabell"). New York: Farrar & Rinehart, 1938
HAMLET HAD AN UNCLE[4] (by "Branch Cabell"). New York: Farrar & Rinehart, 1940
THE FIRST GENTLEMAN OF AMERICA[4] (by "Branch Cabell"). New York: Farrar & Rinehart, 1942. London: Lane, 1942, under the title THE FIRST AMERICAN GENTLEMAN
THERE WERE TWO PIRATES.[5] New York: Farrar, Straus, 1946
THE DEVIL'S OWN DEAR SON.[5] New York: Farrar, Straus, 1949

[1]Included in the Poictesme cycle, BIOGRAPHY OF THE LIFE OF MANUEL
[2]A trilogy: THE WITCH-WOMAN, New York: Farrar, Straus, 1948
[3]A trilogy: THE NIGHTMARE HAS TRIPLETS
[4]A trilogy: HEIRS AND ASSIGNS
[5]With THE ST. JOHNS, written in collaboration with A. J. Hanna, a trilogy: IT HAPPENED IN FLORIDA, New York: Farrar & Rinehart, 1943

ERSKINE [PRESTON] CALDWELL (1903-   )
THE BASTARD. New York: Heron, 1929
POOR FOOL. New York: Rariora, 1930
TOBACCO ROAD. New York: Scribner, 1932
GOD'S LITTLE ACRE. New York: Viking, 1933
JOURNEYMAN. New York: Viking, 1935
TROUBLE IN JULY. New York: Duell, Sloan & Pearce, 1940
ALL NIGHT LONG. New York: Duell, Sloan & Pearce, 1942
GEORGIA BOY. New York: Duell, Sloan & Pearce, 1943

TRAGIC GROUND. New York: Duell, Sloan & Pearce, 1944
A HOUSE IN THE UPLANDS. New York: Duell, Sloan & Pearce, 1946
THE SURE HAND OF GOD. New York: Duell, Sloan & Pearce, 1947
THIS VERY EARTH. New York: Duell, Sloan & Pearce, 1948
A PLACE CALLED ESTHERVILLE. New York: Duell, Sloan & Pearce, 1949
EPISODE IN PALMETTO. New York: Duell, Sloan & Pearce, 1950
A LAMP FOR NIGHTFALL. New York: Duell, Sloan & Pearce; Boston: Little, Brown, 1952
LOVE AND MONEY. New York: Duell, Sloan & Pearce; Boston: Little, Brown, 1954
GRETTA. Boston: Little, Brown, 1955
CLAUDELLE INGLISH. Boston: Little, Brown, 1959. London: Heinemann, 1959, under the title CLAUDELLE
JENNY BY NATURE. New York: Farrar, Straus & Cudahy, 1961
CLOSE TO HOME. New York: Farrar, Straus & Cudahy, 1962
THE LAST NIGHT OF SUMMER. New York: Farrar, Straus, 1963

HORTENSE CALISHER (1911-   )
FALSE ENTRY. Boston: Little, Brown, 1961
TEXTURES OF LIFE. Boston: Little, Brown, 1963
JOURNAL FROM ELLIPSIA. Boston: Little, Brown, 1965

MORLEY [EDWARD] CALLAGHAN (1903-   )
STRANGE FUGITIVE. New York: Scribner, 1928
IT'S NEVER OVER. New York: Scribner, 1930
A BROKEN JOURNEY. New York: Scribner, 1932
SUCH IS MY BELOVED. New York: Scribner, 1934
THEY SHALL INHERIT THE EARTH. New York: Random House, 1935
MORE JOY IN HEAVEN. New York: Random House, 1937
THE VARSITY STORY. Toronto: Macmillan, 1948
THE LOVED AND THE LOST. New York: Macmillan, 1951. *Governor-General's Award, 1952*
THE MANY COLORED COAT. New York: Coward-McCann, 1960
A PASSION IN ROME. New York: Coward-McCann, 1961

[DOROTHEA FRANCES] DOROTHY CANFIELD [FISHER] (1879-1958)
GUNHILD. New York: Holt, 1907
THE SQUIRREL-CAGE. New York: Holt, 1912

THE BENT TWIG. New York: Holt, 1915
THE BRIMMING CUP. New York: Harcourt, Brace, 1921
ROUGH-HEWN. New York: Harcourt, Brace, 1922
THE HOME-MAKER. New York: Harcourt, Brace, 1924
HER SON'S WIFE. New York: Harcourt, Brace, 1926
THE DEEPENING STREAM. New York: Harcourt, Brace, 1930
BONFIRE. New York: Harcourt, Brace, 1933
SEASONED TIMBER. New York: Harcourt, Brace, 1939

GILBERT CANNAN (1884-1955)
PETER HOMUNCULUS. London: Heinemann, 1909
DEVIOUS WAYS. London: Heinemann, 1910
LITTLE BROTHER. London: Heinemann, 1912
ROUND THE CORNER. London: Secker, 1913
OLD MOLE. London: Secker, 1914
YOUNG EARNEST. London: Secker, 1915
THREE PRETTY MEN. London: Methuen, 1916. New York: Doran,
    1916, under the title THREE SONS AND A MOTHER
MENDEL. London: Unwin, 1916
THE STUCCO HOUSE. London: Unwin, 1917
MUMMERY. London: Collins, 1918
PINK ROSES. London: Unwin, 1919
TIME AND ETERNITY. London: Chapman & Hall, 1919
PUGS AND PEACOCKS. London: Hutchinson, 1921
SEMBAL. London: Hutchinson, 1922
ANNETTE AND BENNETT. London: Hutchinson, 1922
THE HOUSE OF PROPHECY. London: Butterworth, 1924

TRUMAN CAPOTE, i.e. TRUMAN STRECKFUS PERSONS (1924-)
OTHER VOICES, OTHER ROOMS. New York: Random House,
    1948
THE GRASS HARP. New York: Random House, 1951

[ARTHUR] JOYCE [LUNEL] CARY (1888-1957)
AISSA SAVED. London: Benn, 1932
AN AMERICAN VISITOR. London: Benn, 1933
THE AFRICAN WITCH. London: Gollancz, 1936
CASTLE CORNER. London: Gollancz, 1938
MISTER JOHNSON. London: Gollancz, 1939
CHARLEY IS MY DARLING. London: Joseph, 1940
A HOUSE OF CHILDREN. London: Joseph, 1941. *James Tait Black
    Memorial Prize, 1942*

HERSELF SURPRISED.[1] London: Joseph, 1941
TO BE A PILGRIM.[1] London: Joseph, 1942
THE HORSE'S MOUTH.[1] London: Joseph, 1944
THE MOONLIGHT. London: Joseph, 1946
A FEARFUL JOY. London: Joseph, 1949
PRISONER OF GRACE.[2] London: Joseph, 1952
EXCEPT THE LORD.[2] London: Joseph, 1953
NOT HONOUR MORE.[2] London: Joseph, 1955
THE CAPTIVE AND THE FREE (unfinished). London: Joseph, 1959

[1]A trilogy: FIRST TRILOGY, New York: Harper, 1958
[2]A trilogy

WILLA [SIBERT] CATHER (1873-1947)

Howells Medal, American Academy of Arts and Letters, 1930. Gold Medal for Fiction, National Institute of Arts and Letters, 1944

ALEXANDER'S BRIDGE. Boston: Houghton Mifflin, 1912
O PIONEERS! Boston: Houghton Mifflin, 1913
THE SONG OF THE LARK. Boston: Houghton Mifflin, 1915
MY ÁNTONIA. Boston: Houghton Mifflin, 1918
ONE OF OURS. New York: Knopf, 1922. *Pulitzer Prize, 1923*
A LOST LADY. New York: Knopf, 1923
THE PROFESSOR'S HOUSE. New York: Knopf, 1925
MY MORTAL ENEMY. New York: Knopf, 1926
DEATH COMES FOR THE ARCHBISHOP. New York: Knopf, 1927. *Howells Medal, 1930*
SHADOWS ON THE ROCK. New York: Knopf, 1931
LUCY GAYHEART. New York: Knopf, 1935
SAPPHIRA AND THE SLAVE GIRL. New York: Knopf, 1940

FRANK CAULDWELL: See FRANCIS [HENRY] KING

[JOHN] DAVID CAUTE (1936-   )

AT FEVER PITCH. London: Deutsch, 1959. *John Llewelyn Rhys Memorial Prize, 1960. Authors' Club First Novel Award, 1960*
COMRADE JACOB. London: Deutsch, 1961
THE DECLINE OF THE WEST. London: Deutsch, 1966

MARY CHALLANS: See MARY RENAULT

W. C. CHAPMAN-MORTIMER: See [WILLIAM CHARLES] CHAPMAN MORTIMER

GERDA CHARLES (-   )
THE TRUE VOICE. London: Eyre & Spottiswoode, 1959
THE CROSSING POINT. London: Eyre & Spottiswoode, 1960
A SLANTING LIGHT. London: Eyre & Spottiswoode, 1963. *James Tait Black Memorial Prize, 1964*

MARY ELLEN CHASE (1887-   )
UPLANDS. Boston: Atlantic Monthly, 1927
MARY PETERS. New York: Macmillan, 1934
SILAS CROCKETT. New York: Macmillan, 1935
DAWN IN LYONESSE. New York: Macmillan, 1938
WINDSWEPT. New York: Macmillan, 1941
THE PLUM TREE. New York: Macmillan, 1949
THE EDGE OF DARKNESS. New York: Norton, 1957
THE LOVELY AMBITION. New York: Norton, 1960
A JOURNEY TO BOSTON: New York: Norton, 1965

DANIEL CHAUCER: See FORD MADOX FORD

JOHN CHEEVER (1912-   )
Howells Medal, American Academy of Arts and Letters, 1965
THE WAPSHOT CHRONICLE. New York: Harper, 1957. *National Book Award, 1958*
THE WAPSHOT SCANDAL. New York: Harper & Row, 1964. *Howells Medal, 1965*

THOMAS WILLES CHITTY: See THOMAS HINDE

RICHARD [THOMAS] CHURCH (1893-   )
OLIVER'S DAUGHTER. London: Dent, 1930
HIGH SUMMER. London: Dent, 1931
THE PRODIGAL FATHER. London: Dent, 1933
THE APPLE OF CONCORD. London: Dent, 1935
THE PORCH.[1] London: Dent, 1937. *Femina-Vie Heureuse Prize, 1938*

THE STRONGHOLD.[1] London: Dent, 1939
THE ROOM WITHIN.[1] London: Dent, 1940
THE SAMPLER. London: Dent, 1942
THE NIGHTINGALE. London: Hutchinson, 1952
THE DANGEROUS YEARS. London: Heinemann, 1956
THE CRAB-APPLE TREE. London: Heinemann, 1959
PRINCE ALBERT. London: Heinemann, 1963
[1]A trilogy

WINSTON CHURCHILL (1871-1947)
THE CELEBRITY. New York: Macmillan, 1898
RICHARD CARVEL. New York: Macmillan, 1899
THE CRISIS. New York: Macmillan, 1901
THE CROSSING. New York: Macmillan, 1904
CONISTON. New York: Macmillan, 1906
MR. CREWE'S CAREER. New York: Macmillan, 1908
A MODERN CHRONICLE. New York: Macmillan, 1910
THE INSIDE OF THE CUP. New York: Macmillan, 1913
A FAR COUNTRY. New York: Macmillan, 1915
THE DWELLING-PLACE OF LIGHT. New York: Macmillan, 1917

WALTER VAN TILBURG CLARK (1909-   )
THE OX-BOW INCIDENT. New York: Random House, 1940
THE CITY OF TREMBLING LEAVES. New York: Random House,
 1945
THE TRACK OF THE CAT. New York: Random House, 1949

ALEX[ANDER] COMFORT (1920-   )
NO SUCH LIBERTY. London: Chapman & Hall, 1941
THE ALMOND TREE. London: Chapman & Hall, 1942
THE POWER HOUSE. London: Routledge, 1944
ON THIS SIDE NOTHING. London: Routledge & Kegan Paul, 1949
A GIANT'S STRENGTH. London: Routledge & Kegan Paul, 1952
COME OUT TO PLAY. London: Eyre & Spottiswoode. 1961

Dame I[VY] COMPTON-BURNETT (1892-   )
DOLORES. Edinburgh: Blackwood, 1911
PASTORS AND MASTERS. London: Cranton, 1925
BROTHERS AND SISTERS. London: Cranton, 1929
MEN AND WIVES. London: Heinemann, 1931
MORE WOMEN THAN MEN. London: Heinemann, 1933

A HOUSE AND ITS HEAD. London: Heinemann, 1935
DAUGHTERS AND SONS. London: Gollancz, 1937
A FAMILY AND A FORTUNE. London: Gollancz, 1939
PARENTS AND CHILDREN. London: Gollancz, 1941
ELDERS AND BETTERS. London: Gollancz, 1944
MANSERVANT AND MAIDSERVANT. London: Gollancz, 1947.
New York: Knopf, 1948, under the title BULLIVANT AND
THE LAMBS
TWO WORLDS AND THEIR WAYS. London: Gollancz, 1949
DARKNESS AND DAY. London: Gollancz, 1951
THE PRESENT AND THE PAST. London: Gollancz, 1953
MOTHER AND SON. London: Gollancz, 1955. *James Tait Black
Memorial Prize, 1956*
A FATHER AND HIS FATE. London: Gollancz, 1957
A HERITAGE AND ITS HISTORY. London: Gollancz, 1959
THE MIGHTY AND THEIR FALL. London: Gollancz, 1961
A GOD AND HIS GIFTS. London: Gollancz, 1963

RICHARD [THOMAS] CONDON (1915-   )
THE OLDEST CONFESSION.[1] New York: Appleton-Century-Crofts,
1958
THE MANCHURIAN CANDIDATE.[1] New York: McGraw-Hill, 1959
SOME ANGRY ANGEL. New York: McGraw-Hill, 1960
A TALENT FOR LOVING. New York: McGraw-Hill, 1961
AN INFINITY OF MIRRORS. New York: Random House, 1964
ANY GOD WILL DO. New York: Random House, 1966
[1]Collected as THE TWO-HEADED READER, New York: Random House, 1966

JOSEPH CONRAD, i.e. JOZEF TEODOR KONRAD NALECZ KORZENIOWSKI (1857-1924)
ALMAYER'S FOLLY. London: Unwin, 1895
AN OUTCAST OF THE ISLANDS. London: Unwin, 1896
THE NIGGER OF THE 'NARCISSUS'. London: Heinemann, 1897.
New York: Dodd, Mead, 1897, under the title THE CHILDREN
OF THE SEA
LORD JIM. Edinburgh: Blackwood, 1900
THE INHERITORS (in collaboration with Ford Madox Hueffer).
London: Heinemann, 1901
ROMANCE (in collaboration with Ford Madox Hueffer). London:
Smith, Elder, 1903
NOSTROMO. London: Harper, 1904
THE SECRET AGENT. London: Methuen, 1907

UNDER WESTERN EYES. London: Methuen, 1911
CHANCE. London: Methuen, 1913
VICTORY. London: Methuen, 1915
THE SHADOW-LINE. London: Dent, 1917
THE ARROW OF GOLD. London: Unwin, 1919
THE RESCUE. London: Dent, 1920
THE ROVER. London: Unwin, 1923
THE NATURE OF A CRIME (in collaboration with Ford Madox Hueffer). London: Duckworth, 1924
SUSPENSE (*unfinished*). London: Dent, 1925
THE SISTERS (*fragment*). New York: Gaige, 1928

WILLIAM COOPER, i.e. H[ARRY] S[UMMERFIELD] HOFF (1910-   )

TRINA.[1] London: Heinemann, 1934. New York: Coward-McCann, 1934, under the title IT HAPPENED IN PRK
RHÉA.[1] London: Heinemann, 1935
LISA.[1] London: Heinemann, 1937
THREE MARRIAGES. London: Heinemann, 1946
SCENES FROM PROVINCIAL LIFE.[2,3] London: Cape, 1950
THE STRUGGLES OF ALBERT WOODS. London: Cape, 1952
THE EVER-INTERESTING TOPIC. London: Cape, 1953
DISQUIET AND PEACE. London: Macmillan, 1956
YOUNG PEOPLE. London: Macmillan, 1958
SCENES FROM MARRIED LIFE.[2,3] London: Macmillan, 1961
MEMOIRS OF A NEW MAN. London: Macmillan, 1966

[1]A trilogy
[2]Parts I and III of a trilogy; the MS of Part II, "Scenes from Metropolitan Life," is at the University of Texas, Austin
[3]Collected as SCENES FROM LIFE, New York: Scribner, 1961
Note: The first four novels appeared under the name H. S. Hoff, the others under the name William Cooper.

DAVID JOHN MOORE CORNWELL: See JOHN LE CARRÉ

BARON CORVO: See FREDERICK [WILLIAM SERAFINO AUSTIN LEWIS MARY] ROLFE

JAMES GOULD COZZENS (1903-   )

Howells Medal, American Academy of Arts and Letters, 1960
CONFUSION. Boston: Brimmer, 1924

MICHAEL SCARLETT. New York: Boni, 1925
COCK PIT. New York: Morrow, 1928
THE SON OF PERDITION. New York: Morrow, 1929
S. S. SAN PEDRO. New York: Harcourt, Brace, 1931
THE LAST ADAM. New York: Harcourt, Brace, 1933. London:
    Longmans, 1933, under the title A CURE OF FLESH
CASTAWAY. New York: Random House, 1934
MEN AND BRETHREN. New York: Harcourt, Brace, 1936
ASK ME TOMORROW. New York: Harcourt, Brace, 1940
THE JUST AND THE UNJUST. New York: Harcourt, Brace, 1942
GUARD OF HONOR. New York: Harcourt, Brace, 1948. *Pulitzer
    Prize, 1949*
BY LOVE POSSESSED. New York: Harcourt, Brace, 1957. *Howells
    Medal, 1960*

A[RCHIBALD] J[OSEPH] CRONIN (1896-   )
HATTER'S CASTLE. London: Gollancz, 1931
THREE LOVES. London: Gollancz, 1932
GRAND CANARY. London: Gollancz, 1933
THE STARS LOOK DOWN. London: Gollancz, 1935
THE CITADEL. London: Gollancz, 1937
THE KEYS OF THE KINGDOM. Boston: Little, Brown, 1941.
    London: Gollancz, 1942
THE GREEN YEARS. Boston: Little, Brown, 1944. London: Gol-
    lancz, 1945
SHANNON'S WAY. London: Gollancz, 1948
THE SPANISH GARDENER. London: Gollancz, 1950
BEYOND THIS PLACE. London: Gollancz, 1953
CRUSADER'S TOMB. London: Gollancz, 1956. Boston: Little,
    Brown, 1956, under the title A THING OF BEAUTY
THE NORTHERN LIGHT. London: Gollancz, 1958
THE JUDAS TREE. London: Gollancz, 1961
A SONG OF SIXPENCE. London: Heinemann, 1964

E[DWARD] E[STLIN] CUMMINGS (1894-1962)
THE ENORMOUS ROOM. New York: Boni & Liveright, 1922
EIMI. New York: Covici-Friede, 1933

E. V. CUNNINGHAM: See HOWARD [MELVIN] FAST

EDWARD DAHLBERG (1900-   )
BOTTOM DOGS. London: Putnam, 1929. New York: Simon &
    Schuster, 1930

FROM FLUSHING TO CALVARY. New York: Harcourt, Brace, 1932
THOSE WHO PERISH. New York: Day, 1934

CLEMENCE DANE, i.e. WINIFRED ASHTON (1888-1965)

REGIMENT OF WOMEN.[1] London: Heinemann, 1917
FIRST THE BLADE. London: Heinemann, 1918
LEGEND.[1] London: Heinemann, 1919
THE BABYONS. London: Heinemann, 1927
ENTER SIR JOHN (in collaboration with Helen Simpson). London: Hodder & Stoughton, 1929
PRINTER'S DEVIL (in collaboration with Helen Simpson). London: Hodder & Stoughton, 1930. New York: Cosmopolitan, 1930, under the title AUTHOR UNKNOWN
BROOME STAGES. London: Heinemann, 1931
RE-ENTER SIR JOHN (in collaboration with Helen Simpson). London: Hodder & Stoughton, 1932
THE MOON IS FEMININE. London: Heinemann, 1938
THE ARROGANT HISTORY OF BEN WHITE. London: Heinemann, 1939
HE BRINGS GREAT NEWS. London: Heinemann, 1944
THE FLOWER GIRLS. London: Joseph, 1954
THE GODSON. London: Joseph, 1964

[1]Collected (with other works) in RECAPTURE, London: Heinemann, 1932

CHRISTOPHER DAVIS (1928-   )

LOST SUMMER. New York: Harcourt, Brace, 1958
FIRST FAMILY. New York: Coward-McCann, 1961. London: Hart-Davis, 1959, under the title SCOTTY
A KIND OF DARKNESS. London: Hart-Davis, 1962
BELMARCH. New York: Viking, 1964
THE SHAMIR OF DACHAU. New York: New American Library, 1966

H[AROLD] L[ENOIR] DAVIS (1896-1960)

HONEY IN THE HORN. New York: Harper, 1935. *Harper Prize, 1935. Pulitzer Prize, 1936*
HARP OF A THOUSAND STRINGS. New York: Morrow, 1947
BEULAH LAND. New York: Morrow, 1949
WINDS OF MORNING. New York: Morrow, 1952
THE DISTANT MUSIC. New York: Morrow, 1957

JENNIFER DAWSON (19 -)

THE HA-HA. London: Blond, 1961. *James Tait Black Memorial Prize, 1962*
FOWLER'S SNARE. London: Blond, 1962
THE COLD COUNTRY. London: Blond, 1966

WALTER [JOHN] DE LA MARE, O.M. (1873-1956)

HENRY BROCKEN. London: Murray, 1904
THE RETURN. London: Arnold, 1910. *Polignac Prize, 1911*
THE THREE MULLA-MULGARS. London: Duckworth, 1910. Reissued as THE THREE ROYAL MONKEYS. London: Faber & Gwyer, 1927
MEMOIRS OF A MIDGET. London: Collins, 1921. *James Tait Black Memorial Prize, 1922*

Note: AT FIRST SIGHT (New York: Gaige, 1928) was published, separately, as a novel in the U. S.; in England it was included in a collection, ON THE EDGE (London: Faber & Faber, 1930).

DENIS DELANEY: See PETER [MORRIS] GREEN

NIGEL DENNIS (1912-)

BOYS AND GIRLS COME OUT TO PLAY. London: Eyre & Spottiswoode, 1949. Boston: Houghton Mifflin, 1949, under the title A SEA CHANGE
CARDS OF IDENTITY. London: Weidenfeld & Nicolson, 1955
A HOUSE IN ORDER. London: Weidenfeld & Nicolson, 1966

PETER DE VRIES (1910-)

BUT WHO WAKES THE BUGLER? Boston: Houghton Mifflin, 1940
THE HANDSOME HEART. New York: Coward-McCann, 1943
ANGELS CAN'T DO BETTER. New York: Coward-McCann, 1944
THE TUNNEL OF LOVE. Boston: Little, Brown, 1954
COMFORT ME WITH APPLES. Boston: Little, Brown, 1956
THE MACKEREL PLAZA. Boston: Little, Brown, 1958
THE TENTS OF WICKEDNESS. Boston: Little, Brown, 1959
THROUGH THE FIELDS OF CLOVER. Boston: Little, Brown, 1961
THE BLOOD OF THE LAMB. Boston: Little, Brown, 1962

REUBEN, REUBEN. Boston: Little, Brown, 1964
LET ME COUNT THE WAYS. Boston: Little, Brown, 1965

ISAK DINESEN, i.e. Baroness KAREN BLIXEN (1885-1962)

THE ANGELIC AVENGERS (by "Pierre Andrézel"). London:
Putnam, 1946
EHRENGARD. London: Joseph, 1963

J[AMES] P[ATRICK] DONLEAVY (1926-   )

THE GINGER MAN. Paris: Olympia, 1955. London: Spearman,
1956. New York: McDowell, Obolensky, 1958 (expurgated)
New York: Delacorte, 1965 (unexpurgated)
A SINGULAR MAN. Boston: Atlantic-Little, Brown, 1963
THE SADDEST SUMMER OF SAMUEL S. New York: Delacorte,
1966

JOHN [RODERIGO] DOS PASSOS (1896-   )

Gold Medal for Fiction, National Institute of Arts and Letters, 1957
ONE MAN'S INITIATION—1917. London: Allen & Unwin, 1920.
New York: Doran, 1922. Reissued as FIRST ENCOUNTER,
New York: Philosophical Library, 1945
THREE SOLDIERS. New York: Doran, 1921
STREETS OF NIGHT. New York: Doran, 1923
MANHATTAN TRANSFER. New York: Harper, 1925
THE 42ND PARALLEL.[1] New York: Harper, 1930
1919.[1] New York: Harcourt, Brace, 1932
THE BIG MONEY.[1] New York: Harcourt, Brace, 1936
ADVENTURES OF A YOUNG MAN.[2] New York: Harcourt, Brace,
1939
NUMBER ONE.[2] Boston: Houghton Mifflin, 1943
THE GRAND DESIGN.[2] Boston: Houghton Mifflin, 1949
CHOSEN COUNTRY. Boston: Houghton Mifflin, 1951
MOST LIKELY TO SUCCEED. Englewood Cliffs, N. J.: Prentice-
Hall, 1954
THE GREAT DAYS. New York: Sagamore, 1958
MIDCENTURY. Boston: Houghton Mifflin, 1961
[1]A trilogy: U. S. A., New York: Harcourt, Brace, 1938
[2]A trilogy: DISTRICT OF COLUMBIA, Boston: Houghton Mifflin, 1952

[GEORGE] NORMAN DOUGLAS (1868-1952)

SOUTH WIND. London: Secker, 1917

THEY WENT. London: Chapman & Hall, 1920
IN THE BEGINNING. Florence: Giuntina, 1927. London: Chatto &
Windus, 1928 (*incomplete*). London: Folio Society, 1953
(*complete*)

MARGARET DRABBLE (1939-   )
A SUMMER BIRD-CAGE. London: Weidenfeld & Nicolson, 1963
THE GARRICK YEAR. London: Weidenfeld & Nicolson, 1964
THE MILLSTONE. London: Weidenfeld & Nicolson, 1965. *John
Llewelyn Rhys Memorial Prize, 1966*

THEODORE [HERMAN ALBERT] DREISER (1871-1945)
Award of Merit Medal for the Novel, American Academy of Arts
and Letters, 1944
SISTER CARRIE. New York: Doubleday, Page, 1900
JENNIE GERHARDT. New York: Harper, 1911
THE FINANCIER.[1] New York: Harper, 1912   ,
THE TITAN.[1] New York: Lane, 1914
THE "GENIUS". New York: Lane, 1915
AN AMERICAN TRAGEDY. New York: Boni & Liveright, 1925
THE BULWARK. Garden City: Doubleday, 1946
THE STOIC.[1] Garden City: Doubleday, 1947
[1]TRILOGY OF DESIRE

ALLEN [STUART] DRURY (1918-   )
ADVISE AND CONSENT.[1] Garden City: Doubleday, 1959.
Pulitzer Prize, 1960
A SHADE OF DIFFERENCE.[1] Garden City: Doubleday, 1962
THAT SUMMER. London: Joseph, 1965. New York: Coward-
McCann, 1966
CAPABLE OF HONOR.[1] Garden City: Doubleday, 1966
[1]A projected tetralogy

ALFRED [LEO] DUGGAN (1903-1964)
KNIGHT WITH ARMOUR. London: Faber & Faber, 1950
CONSCIENCE OF THE KING. London: Faber & Faber, 1951
THE LITTLE EMPERORS. London: Faber & Faber, 1951
THE LADY FOR RANSOM. London: Faber & Faber, 1953
LEOPARDS AND LILIES. London: Faber & Faber, 1954
GOD AND MY RIGHT. London: Faber & Faber, 1955. New York:
Coward-McCann, 1955, under the title MY LIFE FOR MY
SHEEP

WINTER QUARTERS. London: Faber & Faber, 1956
THREE'S COMPANY. London: Faber & Faber, 1958
FOUNDING FATHERS. London: Faber & Faber, 1959. New York: Coward-McCann, 1959, under the title CHILDREN OF THE WOLF
THE CUNNING OF THE DOVE. London: Faber & Faber, 1960
FAMILY FAVOURITES. London: Faber & Faber, 1960
THE KING OF ATHELNEY. London: Faber & Faber. 1961. New York: Pantheon, 1961, under the title THE RIGHT LINE OF CERDIC
LORD GEOFFREY'S FANCY. London: Faber & Faber, 1962
ELEPHANTS AND CASTLES. London: Faber & Faber, 1963. New York: Pantheon, 1963, under the title BESIEGER OF CITIES
COUNT BOHEMOND. London: Faber & Faber, 1964

DAPHNE DU MAURIER (1907-   )
THE LOVING SPIRIT. London: Heinemann, 1931
I'LL NEVER BE YOUNG AGAIN. London: Heinemann, 1932
THE PROGRESS OF JULIUS. London: Heinemann, 1933
JAMAICA INN. London: Gollancz, 1936
REBECCA. London: Gollancz, 1938
FRENCHMAN'S CREEK. London: Gollancz, 1941
HUNGRY HILL. London: Gollancz, 1943
THE KING'S GENERAL. London: Gollancz, 1946
THE PARASITES. London: Gollancz, 1949
MY COUSIN RACHEL. London: Gollancz, 1951
MARY ANNE. London: Gollancz, 1954
THE SCAPEGOAT. London: Gollancz, 1957
CASTLE DOR (completion of an unfinished work by Arthur Quiller-Couch). London: Dent, 1962
THE GLASS-BLOWERS. London: Gollancz, 1963
THE FLIGHT OF THE FALCON. London: Gollancz, 1965

LAWRENCE [GEORGE] DURRELL (1912-   )
PIED PIPER OF LOVERS. London: Cassell, 1935
PANIC SPRING (by "Charles Norden"). London: Faber & Faber, 1937
THE BLACK BOOK. Paris: Obelisk, 1938. New York: Dutton, 1960
CEFALÛ. London: Editions Poetry, 1947. Reissued as THE DARK LABYRINTH, London: Faber & Faber, 1961

JUSTINE.[1] London: Faber & Faber, 1957
BALTHAZAR.[1] London: Faber & Faber, 1958
MOUNTOLIVE.[1] London: Faber & Faber, 1958
CLEA.[1] London: Faber & Faber, 1960
[1]THE ALEXANDRIA QUARTET, London: Faber & Faber, 1962

MICHAEL EAST: See MORRIS [LANGLO] WEST

CYPRIAN [ODIATU DUAKA] EKWENSI (19 -)
PEOPLE OF THE CITY. London: Dakers, 1954
JAGUA NANA. London: Hutchinson, 1961
BURNING GRASS. London: Heinemann, 1962
BEAUTIFUL FEATHERS. London: Hutchinson, 1963
ISKA. London: Hutchinson, 1966

[ANNIE] WINIFRED ELLERMAN: See BRYHER

GEORGE P[AUL] ELLIOTT (1918-)
PARKTILDEN VILLAGE. Boston: Beacon, 1958
DAVID KNUDSEN. New York: Random House, 1962
IN THE WORLD. New York: Viking, 1965

RALPH [WALDO] ELLISON (1914-)
INVISIBLE MAN. New York: Random House, 1952. *National Book Award, 1953*

WALTER ERICSON: See HOWARD FAST

PETER EVERETT (19 -)
A DAY OF DWARFS. London: Spearman, 1962
NEGATIVES. London: Cape, 1964. *Somerset Maugham Award, 1965*
THE FETCH. London: Cape, 1966

JAMES T[HOMAS] FARRELL (1904-)
YOUNG LONIGAN.[1] New York: Vanguard, 1932
GAS-HOUSE McGINTY. New York: Vanguard, 1933
THE YOUNG MANHOOD OF STUDS LONIGAN.[1] New York: Vanguard, 1934
JUDGMENT DAY.[1] New York: Vanguard, 1935
A WORLD I NEVER MADE.[2] New York: Vanguard, 1936

NO STAR IS LOST.[2] New York: Vanguard, 1938
TOMMY GALLAGHER'S CRUSADE. New York: Vanguard, 1939
FATHER AND SON.[2] New York: Vanguard, 1940. London: Routledge, 1943, under the title A FATHER AND HIS SON
ELLEN ROGERS. New York: Vanguard, 1941
MY DAYS OF ANGER.[2] New York: Vanguard, 1943
BERNARD CLARE.[3] New York: Vanguard, 1946. London: Routledge, 1948, under the title BERNARD CLAYRE
THE ROAD BETWEEN.[3] New York: Vanguard, 1949
THIS MAN AND THIS WOMAN. New York: Vanguard, 1951
YET OTHER WATERS.[3] New York: Vanguard, 1952
THE FACE OF TIME.[2] New York: Vanguard, 1953
BOARDING HOUSE BLUES. New York: Paperback Library, 1961
THE SILENCE OF HISTORY.[4] Garden City: Doubleday, 1963
WHAT TIME COLLECTS.[4] Garden City: Doubleday, 1964
LONELY FOR THE FUTURE.[4] Garden City: Doubleday, 1966

[1]A trilogy: STUDS LONIGAN, New York: Vanguard, 1935
[2]The Danny O'Neill series
[3]The Bernard Clare [Carr] series
[4]A projected tetralogy

MICHAEL FARRELL (1899-1962)
THY TEARS MIGHT CEASE. London: Hutchinson, 1963

HOWARD [MELVIN] FAST (1914-   )
TWO VALLEYS. New York: Dial, 1933
STRANGE YESTERDAY. New York: Dodd, Mead, 1934
PLACE IN THE CITY. New York: Harcourt, Brace, 1937
CONCEIVED IN LIBERTY. New York: Simon & Schuster, 1939
THE LAST FRONTIER. New York: Duell, Sloan & Pearce, 1941
THE UNVANQUISHED. New York: Duell, Sloan & Pearce, 1942
CITIZEN TOM PAINE. New York: Duell, Sloan & Pearce, 1943
FREEDOM ROAD. New York: Duell, Sloan & Pearce, 1944
THE AMERICAN. New York: Duell, Sloan & Pearce, 1946
THE CHILDREN. New York: Duell, Sloan & Pearce, 1947
CLARKTON. New York: Duell, Sloan & Pearce, 1947
MY GLORIOUS BROTHERS. Boston: Little, Brown, 1948
THE PROUD AND THE FREE. Boston: Little, Brown, 1950
FALLEN ANGEL (by "Walter Ericson"). Boston: Little, Brown, 1951
SPARTACUS. New York: Citadel, 1952
THE PASSION OF SACCO AND VANZETTI. New York: Blue Heron, 1953
SILAS TIMBERMAN. New York: Blue Heron, 1954

THE STORY OF LOLA GREGG. New York: Blue Heron, 1956
MOSES, PRINCE OF EGYPT. New York: Crown, 1958
THE WINSTON AFFAIR. New York: Crown, 1959
SYLVIA (by "E. V. Cunningham"). Garden City: Doubleday, 1960
APRIL MORNING. New York: Crown, 1961
PHYLLIS (by "E. V. Cunningham"). Garden City: Doubleday, 1962
POWER. Garden City: Doubleday, 1962
ALICE. (by "E. V. Cunningham"). Garden City: Doubleday, 1963
SHIRLEY (by "E. V. Cunningham"). Garden City: Doubleday, 1964
AGRIPPA'S DAUGHTER. Garden City: Doubleday, 1964
LYDIA (by "E. V. Cunningham"). Garden City: Doubleday, 1964
PENELOPE (by "E. V. Cunningham"). Garden City: Doubleday, 1965
TORQUEMADA. Garden City: Doubleday, 1966
HELEN (by "E. V. Cunningham"). Garden City: Doubleday, 1966
MARGIE (by "E. V. Cunningham"). New York: Morrow, 1966

WILLIAM [HARRISON] FAULKNER (1897-1962)
Nobel Prize for Literature, 1949 (awarded in 1950). Howells
    Medal, American Academy of Arts and Letters, 1950. Gold
    Medal for Fiction, National Institute of Arts and Letters, 1962
SOLDIERS' PAY. New York: Boni & Liveright, 1926
MOSQUITOES. New York: Boni & Liveright, 1927
SARTORIS. New York: Harcourt, Brace, 1929
THE SOUND AND THE FURY. New York: Cape & Smith, 1929
AS I LAY DYING. New York: Cape & Smith, 1930
SANCTUARY. New York: Cape & Smith, 1931
LIGHT IN AUGUST. New York: Smith & Haas, 1932
PYLON. New York: Smith & Haas, 1935
ABSALOM, ABSALOM! New York: Random House, 1936
THE UNVANQUISHED. New York: Random House, 1938
THE WILD PALMS. New York: Random House, 1939
THE HAMLET.[1] New York: Random House, 1940
GO DOWN, MOSES. New York: Random House, 1942
INTRUDER IN THE DUST. New York: Random House, 1948
REQUIEM FOR A NUN. New York: Random House, 1951
A FABLE. New York: Random House, 1954. *National Book Award,
    1955. Pulitzer Prize, 1955*
THE TOWN.[1] New York: Random House, 1957
THE MANSION.[1] New York: Random House, 1959
THE REIVERS. New York: Random House, 1962. *Pulitzer Prize,
    1963*
[1] A trilogy: SNOPES

PETER S[TEINAM] FEIBLEMAN (1930-   )
A PLACE WITHOUT TWILIGHT. Cleveland: World, 1958
THE DAUGHTERS OF NECESSITY. Cleveland: World, 1959

EDNA FERBER (1887-   )
DAWN O'HARA. New York: Stokes, 1911
FANNY HERSELF. New York: Stokes, 1917
THE GIRLS. Garden City: Doubleday, Page, 1921
SO BIG. Garden City: Doubleday, Page, 1924. *Pulitzer Prize, 1925*
SHOW BOAT. Garden City: Doubleday, Page, 1926
CIMARRON. Garden City: Doubleday, Doran, 1930
AMERICAN BEAUTY. Garden City: Doubleday, Doran, 1931
COME AND GET IT. Garden City: Doubleday, Doran, 1935
SARATOGA TRUNK. Garden City: Doubleday, Doran, 1941
GREAT SON. Garden City: Doubleday, Doran, 1945
GIANT. Garden City: Doubleday, 1952
ICE PALACE. Garden City: Doubleday, 1958

GABRIEL FIELDING, i.e. ALAN GABRIEL BARNSLEY (1916-   )
BROTHERLY LOVE. London: Hutchinson, 1954
IN THE TIME OF GREENBLOOM. London: Hutchinson, 1956
EIGHT DAYS. London: Hutchinson, 1958
THROUGH STREETS BROAD AND NARROW. London: Hutchinson, 1960
THE BIRTHDAY KING. London: Hutchinson, 1962. *W. H. Smith & Son Literary Award, 1963*
GENTLEMEN IN THEIR SEASON. London: Hutchinson, 1966

[ARTHUR ANNESLEY] RONALD FIRBANK (1886-1926)
VAINGLORY. London: Richards, 1915
INCLINATIONS. London: Richards, 1916
CAPRICE. London: Richards, 1917
VALMOUTH. London: Richards, 1919
SANTAL. London: Richards, 1921
THE FLOWER BENEATH THE FOOT. London: Richards, 1923
PRANCING NIGGER. New York: Brentano's, 1924. London: Brentano's, 1925, under the title SORROW IN SUNLIGHT
CONCERNING THE ECCENTRICITIES OF CARDINAL PIRELLI. London: Richards, 1926
THE ARTIFICIAL PRINCESS. London: Duckworth, 1934
THE NEW RYTHUM (*unfinished*). London: Duckworth, 1962

DOROTHY CANFIELD FISHER: See [DOROTHEA FRANCES] DOROTHY CANFIELD [FISHER]

VARDIS [ALVERO] FISHER (1895-   )

TOILERS OF THE HILLS. Boston: Houghton Mifflin, 1928
DARK BRIDWELL. Boston: Houghton Mifflin, 1931
IN TRAGIC LIFE.[1] Caldwell, Idaho: Caxton; Garden City: Doubleday, Doran, 1932. London: Boriswood, 1934, under the title I SEE NO SIN
PASSIONS SPIN THE PLOT.[1] Caldwell, Idaho: Caxton; Garden City: Doubleday, Doran, 1934
WE ARE BETRAYED.[1] Caldwell, Idaho: Caxton; Garden City: Doubleday, Doran, 1935
NO VILLAIN NEED BE.[1] Caldwell, Idaho: Caxton; Garden City: Doubleday, Doran, 1936
APRIL. Caldwell, Idaho: Caxton; Garden City: Doubleday, Doran, 1937
FORGIVE US OUR VIRTUES. Caldwell, Idaho: Caxton, 1938
CHILDREN OF GOD. New York: Harper, 1939. *Harper Prize, 1939*
CITY OF ILLUSION. New York: Harper, 1941
THE MOTHERS. New York: Vanguard, 1943
DARKNESS AND THE DEEP.[2] New York: Vanguard, 1943
THE GOLDEN ROOMS.[2] New York: Vanguard, 1944
INTIMATIONS OF EVE.[2] New York: Vanguard, 1946
ADAM AND THE SERPENT.[2] New York: Vanguard, 1947
THE DIVINE PASSION.[2] New York: Vanguard, 1948
THE VALLEY OF VISION.[2] New York: Abelard, 1951
THE ISLAND OF THE INNOCENT.[2] New York: Abelard, 1952
PEMMICAN. Garden City: Doubleday, 1956
JESUS CAME AGAIN.[2] Denver: Swallow, 1956
A GOAT FOR AZAZEL.[2] Denver: Swallow, 1956
PEACE LIKE A RIVER.[2] Denver: Swallow, 1957
TALE OF VALOR. Garden City: Doubleday, 1958
MY HOLY SATAN.[2] Denver: Swallow, 1958
ORPHANS IN GETHSEMANE.[2] Denver: Swallow, 1960
MOUNTAIN MEN. New York: Morrow, 1965

[1]The Vridar Hunter tetralogy; incorporated in ORPHANS IN GETHSEMANE
[2]THE TESTAMENT OF MAN

F[RANCIS] SCOTT [KEY] FITZGERALD (1896-1940)

THIS SIDE OF PARADISE. New York: Scribner, 1920
THE BEAUTIFUL AND DAMNED. New York: Scribner, 1922

THE GREAT GATSBY. New York: Scribner, 1925
TENDER IS THE NIGHT. New York: Scribner, 1934
THE LAST TYCOON (*unfinished*). New York: Scribner, 1941

MARTIN [ARCHER] FLAVIN (1883-   )
MR. LITTLEJOHN. New York: Harper, 1940
CORPORAL CAT. New York: Harper, 1941
JOURNEY IN THE DARK. New York: Harper, 1943. *Harper Prize, 1943. Pulitzer Prize, 1944*
THE ENCHANTED. New York: Harper, 1947
CAMERON HILL. New York: Harper, 1957

SHELBY FOOTE (1916-   )
TOURNAMENT. New York: Dial, 1949
FOLLOW ME DOWN. New York: Dial, 1950
LOVE IN A DRY SEASON. New York: Dial, 1951
SHILOH. New York: Dial, 1952
JORDAN COUNTY. New York: Dial, 1954

ESTHER FORBES (1891-   )
O GENTEEL LADY! Boston: Houghton Mifflin, 1926
A MIRROR FOR WITCHES. Boston: Houghton Mifflin, 1928
MISS MARVEL. Boston: Houghton Mifflin, 1935
PARADISE. New York: Harcourt, Brace, 1937
THE GENERAL'S LADY. New York: Harcourt, Brace, 1938
THE RUNNING OF THE TIDE. Boston: Houghton Mifflin, 1948
RAINBOW ON THE ROAD. Boston: Houghton Mifflin, 1954

FORD MADOX FORD, i.e. FORD HERMANN MADOX HUEFFER (1873-1939)
THE SHIFTING OF THE FIRE. London: Unwin, 1892
THE INHERITORS (in collaboration with Joseph Conrad). London: Heinemann, 1901
ROMANCE (in collaboration with Joseph Conrad). London: Smith, Elder, 1903
THE BENEFACTOR. London: Brown, Langham, 1905
THE FIFTH QUEEN.[1] London: Rivers, 1906
PRIVY SEAL.[1] London: Rivers, 1907
AN ENGLISH GIRL. London: Methuen, 1907
THE FIFTH QUEEN CROWNED.[1] London: Nash, 1908
MR. APOLLO. London: Methuen, 1908

THE 'HALF MOON'. London: Nash, 1909
A CALL. London: Chatto & Windus, 1910
THE PORTRAIT. London: Methuen, 1910
THE SIMPLE LIFE LIMITED (by "Daniel Chaucer"). London: Lane, 1911
LADIES WHOSE BRIGHT EYES. London: Constable, 1911
THE PANEL. London: Constable, 1912. Indianapolis: Bobbs-Merrill, 1913, under the title RING FOR NANCY
THE NEW HUMPTY-DUMPTY (by "Daniel Chaucer"). London: Lane, 1912
MR. FLEIGHT. London: Latimer, 1913
THE YOUNG LOVELL. London: Chatto & Windus, 1913
THE GOOD SOLDIER. London: Lane, 1915
THE MARSDEN CASE. London: Duckworth, 1923
SOME DO NOT . . .[2] London: Duckworth, 1924
THE NATURE OF A CRIME (in collaboration with Joseph Conrad). London: Duckworth, 1924
NO MORE PARADES.[2] London: Duckworth, 1925
A MAN COULD STAND UP—.[2] London: Duckworth, 1926
LAST POST.[2] London: Duckworth, 1928. New York: Literary Guild, 1929, under the title THE LAST POST
A LITTLE LESS THAN GODS. London: Duckworth, 1928
WHEN THE WICKED MAN. New York: Liveright, 1931. London: Cape, 1932
THE RASH ACT. London: Cape, 1933
HENRY FOR HUGH. Philadelphia: Lippincott, 1934
VIVE LE ROY. Philadelphia: Lippincott, 1936. London: Allen & Unwin, 1937

[1]A trilogy: THE FIFTH QUEEN, London: Bodley Head, 1962
[2]A tetralogy: PARADE'S END, New York: Knopf, 1950
Note: Beginning with THE MARSDEN CASE (1923) all the novels appeared under the name Ford Madox Ford except THE NATURE OF A CRIME (1924)—a work written (with Conrad) much earlier.

JESSE HILL FORD [JR.] (1928-   )

MOUNTAINS OF GILEAD. Boston: Atlantic-Little, Brown, 1961
THE LIBERATION OF LORD BYRON JONES. Boston: Atlantic-Little, Brown, 1965

C[ECIL] S[COTT] FORESTER (1899-1966)

A PAWN AMONG KINGS. London: Methuen, 1924
THE PAID PIPER. London: Methuen, 1924
PAYMENT DEFERRED. London: Lane, 1926
LOVE LIES DREAMING. London: Lane, 1927

THE WONDERFUL WEEK. London: Lane, 1927. Indianapolis: Bobbs-Merrill, 1927, under the title ONE WONDERFUL WEEK

THE SHADOW OF THE HAWK. London: Lane, 1928. Indianapolis: Bobbs-Merrill, 1928, under the title THE DAUGHTER OF THE HAWK

BROWN ON RESOLUTION. London: Lane, 1929. New York: Putnam, 1929, under the title SINGLE-HANDED

PLAIN MURDER. London: Lane, 1930

TWO-AND-TWENTY. London: Lane, 1931

DEATH TO THE FRENCH. London: Lane, 1932. New York: Readers Club, 1942, under the title RIFLEMAN DODD

THE GUN. London: Lane, 1933

THE PEACEMAKER. London: Heinemann, 1934

THE AFRICAN QUEEN. London: Heinemann, 1935

THE GENERAL. London: Joseph, 1936

THE HAPPY RETURN.[1,3] London: Joseph, 1937. Boston: Little, Brown, 1937, under the title BEAT TO QUARTERS

FLYING COLOURS.[1,4] London: Joseph, 1938. *James Tait Black Memorial Prize, 1939*

A SHIP OF THE LINE.[1,3] London: Joseph, 1938. Boston: Little, Brown, 1938, under the title SHIP OF THE LINE. *James Tait Black Memorial Prize, 1939*

THE EARTHLY PARADISE. London: Joseph, 1940. Boston: Little, Brown, 1940, under the title TO THE INDIES

THE CAPTAIN FROM CONNECTICUT. London: Joseph, 1941

THE SHIP. London: Joseph, 1943

THE COMMODORE.[4] London: Joseph, 1945. Boston: Little, Brown, 1945, under the title COMMODORE HORNBLOWER

LORD HORNBLOWER.[4] London: Joseph, 1946

THE SKY AND THE FOREST. London: Joseph, 1948

MR. MIDSHIPMAN HORNBLOWER.[2] London: Joseph, 1950

RANDALL AND THE RIVER OF TIME. London: Joseph, 1951

LIEUTENANT HORNBLOWER.[2] London: Joseph, 1952

HORNBLOWER AND THE ATROPOS.[2] London: Joseph, 1953

THE GOOD SHEPHERD. London: Joseph, 1955

ADMIRAL HORNBLOWER IN THE WEST INDIES.[4] London: Joseph, 1958

HORNBLOWER AND THE HOTSPUR.[3] London: Joseph, 1962

[1] A trilogy: CAPTAIN HORNBLOWER, R.N., London: Joseph, 1939; under the title CAPTAIN HORATIO HORNBLOWER, Boston: Little, Brown, 1939

[2] A trilogy: THE YOUNG HORNBLOWER, London: Joseph, 1964

[3] A trilogy: CAPTAIN HORNBLOWER, R.N., London: Joseph, 1965

[4] A tetralogy: ADMIRAL HORNBLOWER, London: Joseph, 1966

E[DWARD] M[ORGAN] FORSTER, C. Litt. (1879-   )

WHERE ANGELS FEAR TO TREAD. Edinburgh: Blackwood, 1905
THE LONGEST JOURNEY. Edinburgh: Blackwood, 1907
A ROOM WITH A VIEW. London: Arnold, 1908
HOWARDS END. London: Arnold, 1910
A PASSAGE TO INDIA. London: Arnold, 1924. *James Tait Black Memorial Prize, 1925. Femina-Vie Heureuse Prize, 1925*

JOHN FOWLES (1926-   )

THE COLLECTOR. London: Cape, 1963
THE MAGUS. London: Cape, 1966

JANET [PATERSON] FRAME [CLUTHA] (1924-   )

OWLS DO CRY. Christchurch, N.Z.: Pegasus, 1957
FACES IN THE WATER. Christchurch, N.Z.: Pegasus, 1961
THE EDGE OF THE ALPHABET. Christchurch, N.Z.: Pegasus, 1962
SCENTED GARDENS FOR THE BLIND. Christchurch, N.Z.: Pegasus, 1963
THE ADAPTABLE MAN. London: Allen, 1965
A STATE OF SIEGE. New York: Braziller, 1966

MICHAEL FRAYN (1933-   )

THE TIN MEN. London: Collins, 1965. *Somerset Maugham Award, 1966*
THE RUSSIAN INTERPRETER. London: Collins, 1966. *Hawthornden Prize, 1967*

BRUCE JAY FRIEDMAN (1930-   )

STERN. New York: Simon & Schuster, 1962
A MOTHER'S KISSES. New York: Simon & Schuster, 1964

DANIEL FUCHS (1909-   )

SUMMER IN WILLIAMSBURG. New York: Vanguard, 1934
HOMAGE TO BLENHOLT. New York: Vanguard, 1936
LOW COMPANY. New York: Vanguard, 1937. London: Constable, 1937, under the title NEPTUNE BEACH

ROY [BROADBENT] FULLER (1912-   )

THE SECOND CURTAIN. London: Verschoyle, 1953

FANTASY AND FUGUE. London: Verschoyle, 1954
IMAGE OF A SOCIETY. London: Deutsch, 1956
THE RUINED BOYS. London: Deutsch, 1959. New York: Macmillan, 1959, under the title THAT DISTANT AFTERNOON
THE FATHER'S COMEDY. London: Deutsch, 1961
THE PERFECT FOOL. London: Deutsch, 1963
MY CHILD, MY SISTER. London: Deutsch, 1965

WILLIAM GADDIS (1922-   )
THE RECOGNITIONS. New York: Harcourt, Brace, 1955

ZONA GALE (1874-1938)
ROMANCE ISLAND. Indianapolis: Bobbs-Merrill, 1906
MOTHERS TO MEN. New York: Macmillan, 1911
CHRISTMAS. New York: Macmillan, 1912
HEART'S KINDRED. New York: Macmillan, 1915
A DAUGHTER OF THE MORNING. Indianapolis: Bobbs-Merrill, 1917
BIRTH. New York: Macmillan, 1918
MISS LULU BETT. New York: Appleton, 1920
FAINT PERFUME. New York: Appleton, 1923
PREFACE TO A LIFE. New York: Appleton, 1926
BORGIA. New York: Knopf, 1929
PAPA LA FLEUR. New York: Appleton, 1933
LIGHT WOMAN. New York: Appleton-Century, 1937
MAGNA. New York: Appleton-Century, 1939

JOHN GALSWORTHY, O.M. (1867-1933)
Nobel Prize for Literature, 1932
JOCELYN (by "John Sinjohn"). London: Duckworth, 1898
VILLA RUBEIN (by "John Sinjohn"). London: Duckworth, 1900
THE ISLAND PHARISEES. London: Heinemann, 1904
THE MAN OF PROPERTY.[1] London: Heinemann, 1906
THE COUNTRY HOUSE. London: Heinemann, 1907
FRATERNITY. London: Heinemann, 1909
THE PATRICIAN. London: Heinemann, 1911
THE DARK FLOWER. London: Heinemann, 1913
THE FREELANDS. London: Heinemann, 1915
BEYOND. London: Heinemann, 1917
THE BURNING SPEAR (by "A. R. P—m"). London: Chatto & Windus, 1919
SAINT'S PROGRESS. London: Heinemann, 1919

IN CHANCERY.[1] London: Heinemann, 1920
TO LET.[1] London: Heinemann, 1921
THE WHITE MONKEY.[2] London: Heinemann, 1924
THE SILVER SPOON.[2] London: Heinemann, 1926
SWAN SONG.[2] London: Heinemann, 1928
MAID IN WAITING.[3] London: Heinemann, 1931
FLOWERING WILDERNESS.[3] London: Heinemann, 1932
OVER THE RIVER.[3] London: Heinemann, 1933. New York: Scribner, 1933, under the title ONE MORE RIVER

[1]A trilogy: THE FORSYTE SAGA, London: Heinemann, 1922
[2]A trilogy: A MODERN COMEDY, London: Heinemann, 1929
[3]A trilogy: END OF THE CHAPTER, New York: Scribner, 1934; London: Heinemann, 1935

DAVID GARNETT (1892-   )

DOPE-DARLING (by "Leda Burke"). London: Laurie, 1919
LADY INTO FOX. London: Chatto & Windus, 1922. *James Tait Black Memorial Prize, 1923. Hawthornden Prize, 1923*
A MAN IN THE ZOO. London: Chatto & Windus, 1924
THE SAILOR'S RETURN. London: Chatto & Windus, 1925
GO SHE MUST! London: Chatto & Windus, 1927
NO LOVE. London: Chatto & Windus, 1929
THE GRASSHOPPERS COME. London: Chatto & Windus, 1931
POCAHONTAS. London: Chatto & Windus, 1933
BEANY-EYE. London: Chatto & Windus, 1935
ASPECTS OF LOVE. London: Chatto & Windus, 1955
A SHOT IN THE DARK. London: Longmans, 1958
A NET FOR VENUS. London: Longmans, 1959
TWO BY TWO. London: Longmans, 1963
ULTERIOR MOTIVES. London: Longmans, 1966

GEORGE [PALMER] GARRETT [JR.] (1929-   )

THE FINISHED MAN. New York: Scribner, 1959
WHICH ARE THE ENEMY? Boston: Little, Brown, 1961
DO, LORD, REMEMBER ME. Garden City: Doubleday, 1965

WILLIAM [ALEXANDER] GERHARDT (1895-   )

FUTILITY. London: Cobden-Sanderson, 1922
THE POLYGLOTS. London: Cobden-Sanderson, 1925
JAZZ AND JASPER. London: Duckworth, 1928. New York: Duffield, 1928, under the title EVA'S APPLES. Reissued as MY

SINFUL EARTH, London: Macdonald, 1947
PENDING HEAVEN. London: Duckworth, 1930
THE MEMOIRS OF SATAN (in collaboration with Brian Lunn).
    London: Cassell, 1932
RESURRECTION. London: Cassell, 1934
OF MORTAL LOVE. London: Barker, 1936
MY WIFE'S THE LEAST OF IT. London: Faber & Faber, 1938

LEWIS GRASSIC GIBBON, i.e.   J[AMES] LESLIE MITCHELL (1901-1935)

STAINED RADIANCE. London: Jarrolds, 1930
THE THIRTEENTH DISCIPLE. London: Jarrolds, 1931
THREE GO BACK. London: Jarrolds, 1932
THE LOST TRUMPET. London: Jarrolds, 1932
SUNSET SONG.[1] London: Jarrolds, 1932
IMAGE AND SUPERSCRIPTION. London: Jarrolds, 1933
CLOUD HOWE.[1] London: Jarrolds, 1933
SPARTACUS. London: Jarrolds, 1933
GAY HUNTER. London: Heinemann, 1934
GREY GRANITE.[1] London: Jarrolds, 1934

[1]A trilogy: A SCOTS QUAIR, London: Jarrolds, 1946. Only this work and
    its component parts were published under the name Lewis Grassic Gibbon.

STELLA [DOROTHEA] GIBBONS (1902-   )

COLD COMFORT FARM. London: Longmans, 1932. *Femina-Vie
    Heureuse Prize, 1934*
BASSETT. London: Longmans, 1934
ENBURY HEATH. London: Longmans, 1935
MISS LINSEY AND PA. London: Longmans, 1936
NIGHTINGALE WOOD. London: Longmans, 1938
MY AMERICAN. London: Longmans, 1939
THE RICH HOUSE. London: Longmans, 1941
TICKY. London: Longmans, 1943
THE BACHELOR. London: Longmans, 1944
WESTWOOD. London: Longmans, 1946. New York: Dodd, Mead,
    1946, under the title THE GENTLE POWERS
THE MATCHMAKER. London: Longmans, 1949
CONFERENCE AT COLD COMFORT FARM. London: Longmans,
    1949
THE SWISS SUMMER. London: Longmans, 1951
FORT OF THE BEAR. London: Longmans, 1953
THE SHADOW OF A SORCERER. London: Hodder & Stoughton,
    1955

HERE BE DRAGONS. London: Hodder & Stoughton, 1956
WHITE SAND AND GREY SAND. London: Hodder & Stoughton, 1958
A PINK FRONT DOOR. London: Hodder & Stoughton, 1959
THE WEATHER AT TREGULLA. London: Hodder & Stoughton, 1962
THE WOLVES WERE IN THE SLEDGE. London: Hodder & Stoughton, 1964
THE CHARMERS. London: Hodder & Stoughton, 1965

BRIAN [LESTER] GLANVILLE (1931-   )
THE RELUCTANT DICTATOR. London: Laurie, 1952
HENRY SOWS THE WIND. London: Secker & Warburg, 1954
ALONG THE ARNO. London: Secker & Warburg, 1956
THE BANKRUPTS. London: Secker & Warburg, 1958
AFTER ROME, AFRICA. London: Secker & Warburg, 1959
DIAMOND. London: Secker & Warburg, 1962
THE RISE OF GERRY LOGAN. London: Secker & Warburg, 1963
A SECOND HOME. London: Secker & Warburg, 1965
A ROMAN MARRIAGE. London: Joseph, 1966

ELLEN [ANDERSON GHOLSON] GLASGOW (1873-1945)
Howells Medal, American Academy of Arts and Letters, 1940
THE DESCENDANT (Anonymous). New York: Harper, 1897
PHASES OF AN INFERIOR PLANET. New York: Harper, 1898
THE VOICE OF THE PEOPLE. New York: Doubleday, Page, 1900
THE BATTLE-GROUND. New York: Doubleday, Page, 1902
THE DELIVERANCE. New York: Doubleday, Page, 1904
THE WHEEL OF LIFE. New York: Doubleday, Page, 1906
THE ANCIENT LAW. New York: Doubleday, Page, 1908
THE ROMANCE OF A PLAIN MAN. New York: Macmillan, 1909
THE MILLER OF OLD CHURCH. Garden City: Doubleday, Page, 1911
VIRGINIA. Garden City: Doubleday, Page, 1913
LIFE AND GABRIELLA. Garden City: Doubleday, Page, 1916
THE BUILDERS. Garden City: Doubleday, Page, 1919
ONE MAN IN HIS TIME. Garden City: Doubleday, Page, 1922
BARREN GROUND. Garden City: Doubleday, Page, 1925
THE ROMANTIC COMEDIANS. Garden City: Doubleday, Page, 1926
THEY STOOPED TO FOLLY. Garden City: Doubleday, Doran, 1929

THE SHELTERED LIFE. Garden City: Doubleday, Doran, 1932
VEIN OF IRON. New York: Harcourt, Brace, 1935
IN THIS OUR LIFE. New York: Harcourt, Brace, 1941. *Pulitzer Prize, 1942*
BEYOND DEFEAT. Charlottesville: Virginia, 1966

G[ERALD] M[ARCUS] GLASKIN (1924-   )
A WORLD OF OUR OWN. London: Barrie, 1955
A MINOR PORTRAIT. London: Barrie, 1957
A CHANGE OF MIND. London: Barrie & Rockliff, 1959
A LION IN THE SUN. London: Barrie & Rockliff, 1960
THE BEACH OF PASSIONATE LOVE. London: Barrie & Rockliff, 1961
A WALTZ THROUGH THE HILLS. London: Barrie & Rockliff, 1961
FLIGHT TO LANDFALL. London: Barrie & Rockliff, 1963
THE MAN WHO DIDN'T COUNT. London: Barrie & Rockliff, 1965

SUSAN GLASPELL (1882-1948)
THE GLORY OF THE CONQUERED. New York: Stokes, 1909
THE VISIONING. New York: Stokes, 1911
FIDELITY. Boston: Small, Maynard, 1915
BROOK EVANS. New York: Stokes, 1928
FUGITIVE'S RETURN. New York: Stokes, 1929
AMBROSE HOLT AND FAMILY. New York: Stokes, 1931
THE MORNING IS NEAR US. New York: Stokes, 1940
NORMA ASHE. Philadelphia: Lippincott, 1942
JUDD RANKIN'S DAUGHTER. Philadelphia: Lippincott, 1945. London: Gollancz, 1946, under the title PRODIGAL GIVER

JON GODDEN (1906-   )
THE BIRD ESCAPED. New York: Rinehart, 1947
THE HOUSE BY THE SEA. London: Joseph, 1947
THE PEACOCK. London: Joseph, 1950
THE CITY AND THE WAVE. London: Joseph, 1954
THE SEVEN ISLANDS. London: Chatto & Windus, 1956
MRS. PANOPOULIS. London: Chatto & Windus, 1959
TOLD IN WINTER. London: Chatto & Windus, 1961. New York: Knopf, 1961, under the title A WINTER'S TALE
IN THE SUN. London: Chatto & Windus, 1965

[MARGARET] RUMER GODDEN (1907-   )

CHINESE PUZZLE. London: Davies, 1936
THE LADY AND THE UNICORN. London: Davies, 1937
BLACK NARCISSUS. London: Davies, 1939
GYPSY, GYPSY. London: Davies, 1940
BREAKFAST WITH THE NIKOLIDES. London: Davies, 1942
A FUGUE IN TIME. London: Joseph, 1945. Boston: Little, Brown, 1945, under the title TAKE THREE TENSES
THE RIVER. London: Joseph, 1946
A CANDLE FOR ST. JUDE. London: Joseph, 1948
A BREATH OF AIR. London: Joseph, 1950
KINGFISHERS CATCH FIRE. London: Macmillan, 1953
AN EPISODE OF SPARROWS. New York: Viking, 1955. London: Macmillan, 1956
THE GREENGAGE SUMMER. London: Macmillan, 1958
CIIINA COURT. London: Macmillan, 1961
THE BATTLE OF THE VILLA FIORITA. London: Macmillan, 1963

HERBERT GOLD (1924-   )

BIRTH OF A HERO. New York: Viking, 1951
THE PROSPECT BEFORE US. Cleveland: World, 1954
THE MAN WHO WAS NOT WITH IT. Boston: Atlantic-Little, Brown, 1956
THE OPTIMIST. Boston: Atlantic-Little, Brown, 1959
THEREFORE BE BOLD. New York: Dial, 1960
SALT. New York: Dial, 1963

LOUIS GOLDING (1895-1958)

FORWARD FROM BABYLON. London: Christophers, 1920
SEACOAST OF BOHEMIA. London: Christophers, 1923
DAY OF ATONEMENT. London: Chatto & Windus, 1925
STORE OF LADIES. London: Knopf, 1927
THE MIRACLE BOY. London: Knopf, 1927
THE PRINCE OR SOMEBODY. London: Knopf, 1929
GIVE UP YOUR LOVERS. London: Heinemann, 1930
MAGNOLIA STREET. London: Gollancz, 1932
FIVE SILVER DAUGHTERS. London: Gollancz, 1934
THE CAMBERWELL BEAUTY. London: Gollancz, 1935
THE PURSUER. London: Gollancz, 1936
THE DANCE GOES ON. London: Rich & Cowan, 1937
MR. EMMANUEL. London: Rich & Cowan, 1939

WHO'S THERE WITHIN? London: Hutchinson, 1942
NO NEWS FROM HELEN. London: Hutchinson, 1943
THE GLORY OF ELSIE SILVER. London: Hutchinson, 1945
THREE JOLLY GENTLEMEN. London: Hutchinson, 1947
HONEY FOR THE GHOST. London: Hutchinson, 1949
THE DANGEROUS PLACES. London: Hutchinson, 1951
THE LOVING BROTHERS. London: Hutchinson, 1952
TO THE QUAYSIDE. London: Hutchinson, 1954
MR. HURRICANE. London: Hutchinson, 1957
THE LITTLE OLD ADMIRAL. London: Hutchinson, 1958

WILLIAM [GERALD] GOLDING (1911-   )
LORD OF THE FLIES. London: Faber & Faber, 1954
THE INHERITORS. London: Faber & Faber, 1955
PINCHER MARTIN. London: Faber & Faber, 1956. New York:
    Harcourt, Brace, 1957, under the title THE TWO DEATHS
    OF CHRISTOPHER MARTIN
FREE FALL. London: Faber & Faber, 1959
THE SPIRE. London: Faber & Faber, 1964

NADINE GORDIMER (1923-   )
THE LYING DAYS. London: Gollancz, 1953
A WORLD OF STRANGERS. London: Gollancz, 1958
OCCASION FOR LOVING. London: Gollancz, 1963
THE LATE BOURGEOIS WORLD. London: Gollancz, 1966

CAROLINE GORDON (1895-   )
PENHALLY. New York: Scribner, 1931
ALECK MAURY, SPORTSMAN. New York: Scribner, 1934
NONE SHALL LOOK BACK. New York: Scribner, 1937
THE GARDEN OF ADONIS. New York: Scribner, 1937
GREEN CENTURIES. New York: Scribner, 1941
THE WOMEN ON THE PORCH. New York: Scribner, 1944
THE STRANGE CHILDREN. New York: Scribner, 1951
THE MALEFACTORS. New York: Harcourt, Brace, 1956

[CHARLES] WILLIAM GOYEN (1915-   )
THE HOUSE OF BREATH. New York: Random House, 1950
IN A FARTHER COUNTRY. New York: Random House, 1955
THE FAIR SISTER. Garden City: Doubleday, 1963. London:
    Owen, 1963, under the title SAVATA, MY FAIR SISTER

SHIRLEY ANN GRAU (1929-   )
THE HARD BLUE SKY. New York: Knopf, 1958
THE HOUSE ON COLISEUM STREET. New York: Knopf, 1961
THE KEEPERS OF THE HOUSE. New York: Knopf, 1964. *Pulitzer Prize, 1965*

ROBERT [VON RANKE] GRAVES (1895-   )
MY HEAD! MY HEAD! London: Secker, 1925
NO DECENCY LEFT (in collaboration with Laura Riding; by "Barbara Rich"). London: Cape, 1932
I, CLAUDIUS. London: Barker, 1934. *James Tait Black Memorial Prize, 1935. Hawthornden Prize, 1935*
CLAUDIUS THE GOD. London: Barker, 1934. *James Tait Black Memorial Prize, 1935*
ANTIGUA, PENNY, PUCE. London: Constable, 1936. New York: Random House, 1936, under the title THE ANTIGUA STAMP
COUNT BELISARIUS. London: Cassell, 1938. *Femina-Vie Heureuse Prize, 1939*
SERGEANT LAMB OF THE NINTH. London: Methuen, 1940. New York: Random House, 1940, under the title SERGEANT LAMB'S AMERICA
PROCEED, SERGEANT LAMB. London: Methuen, 1941
THE STORY OF MARIE POWELL. London: Cassell, 1943. New York: Creative Age, 1944, under the title WIFE TO MR. MILTON
THE GOLDEN FLEECE. London: Cassell, 1944. New York: Creative Age, 1945, under the title HERCULES, MY SHIPMATE
KING JESUS. London: Cassell, 1946
SEVEN DAYS IN NEW CRETE. London: Cassell, 1949. New York: Creative Age, 1949, under the title WATCH THE NORTH WIND RISE
THE ISLES OF UNWISDOM. London: Cassell, 1950. Garden City: Doubleday, 1949, under the title THE ISLANDS OF UNWISDOM
HOMER'S DAUGHTER. London: Cassell, 1955
THEY HANGED MY SAINTLY BILLY. London: Cassell, 1957

HENRY GREEN, i.e. HENRY VINCENT YORKE (1905-   )
BLINDNESS. London: Dent, 1926
LIVING. London: Dent, 1929
PARTY GOING. London: Hogarth, 1939

CAUGHT. London: Hogarth, 1943
LOVING. London: Hogarth, 1945
BACK. London: Hogarth, 1946
CONCLUDING. London: Hogarth, 1948
NOTHING. London: Hogarth, 1950
DOTING. London: Hogarth, 1952

PAUL [ELIOT] GREEN (1894-   )
THE LAUGHING PIONEER. New York: McBride, 1932
THIS BODY THE EARTH. New York: Harper, 1935

PETER [MORRIS] GREEN (1924-   )
ACHILLES HIS ARMOUR. London: Murray, 1955
CAT IN GLOVES (by "Denis Delaney"). London: Gryphon Books, 1956
THE SWORD OF PLEASURE. London: Murray, 1957. *Heinemann Award, 1958*
THE LAUGHTER OF APHRODITE. London: Murray, 1965

[HENRY] GRAHAM GREENE (1904-   )
THE MAN WITHIN. London: Heinemann, 1929
THE NAME OF ACTION. London: Heinemann, 1930
RUMOUR AT NIGHTFALL. London: Heinemann, 1931
STAMBOUL TRAIN. London: Heinemann, 1932. Garden City: Doubleday, Doran, 1933, under the title ORIENT EXPRESS
IT'S A BATTLEFIELD. London: Heinemann, 1934
ENGLAND MADE ME. London: Heinemann, 1935. New York: Viking, 1953, under the title THE SHIPWRECKED
A GUN FOR SALE.[1] London: Heinemann, 1936. Garden City: Doubleday, Doran, 1936, under the title THIS GUN FOR HIRE
BRIGHTON ROCK. London: Heinemann, 1938
THE CONFIDENTIAL AGENT.[1] London: Heinemann, 1939
THE POWER AND THE GLORY. London: Heinemann, 1940. New York: Viking, 1940, under the title THE LABYRINTHINE WAYS. *Hawthornden Prize, 1941*
THE MINISTRY OF FEAR.[1] London: Heinemann, 1943
THE HEART OF THE MATTER. London: Heinemann, 1948. *James Tait Black Memorial Prize, 1949*
THE THIRD MAN.[2] New York: Viking, 1950
THE END OF THE AFFAIR. London: Heinemann, 1951
LOSER TAKES ALL. London: Heinemann, 1955

THE QUIET AMERICAN. London: Heinemann, 1955
OUR MAN IN HAVANA. London: Heinemann, 1958
A BURNT-OUT CASE.[3] London: Heinemann, 1961
THE COMEDIANS. London: Bodley Head, 1966

[1]Collected as THREE, New York: Viking, 1952
[2]Issued separately only in the U. S.; published in England with THE FALLEN
   IDOL, London: Heinemann, 1950
[3]First published in translation under the title UTBRAND, Stockholm: Norstedt,
   1960

GWYN GRIFFIN (1922-   )

THE OCCUPYING POWER. Sydney: Angus & Robertson, 1956
BY THE NORTH GATE. Sydney: Angus & Robertson, 1958
SONS OF GOD. London: Angus & Robertson, 1960. New York:
    Holt, 1960, under the title SOMETHING OF AN ACHIEVE-
    MENT
SHIPMASTER. London: Collins, 1961. New York: Holt, Rinehart &
    Winston, 1961, under the title MASTER OF THIS VESSEL
FREEDOM OBSERVED. London: Collins, 1963
A SIGNIFICANT EXPERIENCE. New York: Holt, Rinehart &
    Winston, 1963. London: Collins, 1964
A LAST LAMP BURNING. London: Collins, 1966

DAVIS [ALEXANDER] GRUBB (1919-   )

THE NIGHT OF THE HUNTER. New York: Harper, 1953
A DREAM OF KINGS. New York: Scribner, 1955
THE WATCHMAN. New York: Scribner, 1961
THE VOICES OF GLORY. New York: Scribner, 1962
A TREE FULL OF STARS. New York: Scribner, 1965
SHADOW OF MY BROTHER. New York: Holt, Rinehart & Wins-
    ton, 1966

NEIL M[ILLER] GUNN (1891-   )

THE GREY COAST. London: Cape, 1926
MORNING TIDE. Edinburgh: Porpoise, 1931
THE LOST GLEN. Edinburgh: Porpoise, 1932
SUN CIRCLE. Edinburgh: Porpoise, 1933
BUTCHER'S BROOM. Edinburgh: Porpoise, 1934
HIGHLAND RIVER. Edinburgh: Porpoise, 1937. *James Tait Black
    Memorial Prize, 1938*
WILD GEESE OVERHEAD. London: Faber & Faber, 1939
SECOND SIGHT. London: Faber & Faber, 1940
THE SILVER DARLINGS. London: Faber & Faber, 1941

YOUNG ART AND OLD HECTOR. London: Faber & Faber, 1942
THE SERPENT. London: Faber & Faber, 1943. New York: Stewart, 1944, under the title MAN GOES ALONE
THE GREEN ISLE OF THE GREAT DEEP. London: Faber & Faber, 1944
THE KEY OF THE CHEST. London: Faber & Faber, 1945
THE DRINKING WELL. London: Faber & Faber, 1946
THE SHADOW. London: Faber & Faber, 1948
THE SILVER BOUGH. London: Faber & Faber, 1948
THE LOST CHART. London: Faber & Faber, 1949
THE WELL AT THE WORLD'S END. London: Faber & Faber, 1951
BLOODHUNT. London: Faber & Faber, 1952
THE OTHER LANDSCAPE. London: Faber & Faber, 1954

A[LFRED] B[ERTRAM] GUTHRIE, JR. (1901-   )
THE BIG SKY. New York: Sloane, 1947
THE WAY WEST. New York: Sloane, 1949. *Pulitzer Prize, 1950*
THESE THOUSAND HILLS. Boston: Houghton Mifflin, 1956

NANCY HALE (1908-   )
THE YOUNG DIE GOOD. New York: Scribner, 1932
NEVER ANY MORE. New York: Scribner, 1934
THE PRODIGAL WOMEN. New York: Scribner, 1942
THE SIGN OF JONAH. New York: Scribner, 1950
HEAVEN AND HARDPAN FARM. New York: Scribner, 1957
DEAR BEAST. Boston: Little, Brown, 1959
BLACK SUMMER. Boston: Little, Brown, 1963

[MARGUERITE] RADCLYFFE HALL (1886-1943)
THE FORGE. London: Arrowsmith, 1924
THE UNLIT LAMP. London: Cassell, 1924
A SATURDAY LIFE. London: Arrowsmith, 1925
ADAM'S BREED. London: Cassell, 1926. *James Tait Black Memorial Prize, 1927. Femina-Vie Heureuse Prize, 1927*
THE WELL OF LONELINESS. London: Cape, 1928
THE MASTER OF THE HOUSE. London: Cape, 1932
THE SIXTH BEATITUDE. London: Heinemann, 1936

[SAMUEL] DASHIELL HAMMETT (1894-1961)
RED HARVEST. New York: Knopf, 1929

THE DAIN CURSE. New York: Knopf, 1929
THE MALTESE FALCON. New York: Knopf, 1930
THE GLASS KEY. New York: Knopf, 1931
THE THIN MAN. New York: Knopf, 1932
TULIP (*fragment*), in THE BIG KNOCKOVER. New York: Random House, 1966. London: Cassell, 1966, in THE DASHIELL HAMMETT STORY OMNIBUS

GERALD [ANTHONY] HANLEY (1916-   )
THE CONSUL AT SUNSET. London: Collins, 1951
THE YEAR OF THE LION. London: Collins, 1953
DRINKERS OF DARKNESS. London: Collins, 1955
WITHOUT LOVE. London: Collins, 1957
THE HOMEWARD JOURNEY. London: Collins, 1961
GILLIGAN'S LAST ELEPHANT. London: Collins, 1962

JAMES HANLEY (1901-   )
DRIFT. London: Partridge, 1930
BOY. London: Boriswood, 1931
EBB AND FLOOD. London. Lane, 1932
CAPTAIN BOTTELL. London: Boriswood, 1933
RESURREXIT DOMINUS. London: Privately printed, 1934
THE FURYS.[1] London: Chatto & Windus, 1935
STOKER BUSH. London: Chatto & Windus, 1935
THE SECRET JOURNEY.[1] London: Chatto & Windus, 1936
HOLLOW SEA. London: Lane, 1938
OUR TIME IS GONE.[1] London: Lane, 1940
THE OCEAN. London: Faber & Faber, 1941
NO DIRECTIONS. London: Faber & Faber, 1943
SAILOR'S SONG. London: Nicholson & Watson, 1943
WHAT FARRAR SAW. London: Nicholson & Watson, 1946
EMILY. London: Nicholson & Watson, 1948
WINTER SONG.[1] London: Pheonix House, 1950
THE HOUSE IN THE VALLEY (by "Patric Shone"). London: Cape, 1951
THE CLOSED HARBOUR. London: Macdonald, 1952
THE WELSH SONATA. London: Verschoyle, 1954
LEVINE. London: Macdonald, 1956
AN END AND A BEGINNING.[1] London: Macdonald, 1958
SAY NOTHING. London: Macdonald, 1962
[1]The Fury sequence

RONALD [HAROLD] HARDY (1919-   )

THE PLACE OF JACKALS. London: Muller, 1954
A NAME LIKE HEROD. London: Muller, 1955
KAMPONG. London: Muller, 1957
THE MEN FROM THE BUSH. London: Muller, 1959
ACT OF DESTRUCTION. London: Weidenfeld & Nicolson, 1962. *James Tait Black Memorial Prize, 1963*

MARK HARRIS (1922-   )

TRUMPET TO THE WORLD. New York: Reynal & Hitchcock, 1946
THE SOUTHPAW. Indianapolis: Bobbs-Merrill, 1953
BANG THE DRUM SLOWLY. New York: Knopf, 1956
A TICKET FOR A SEAMSTITCH. New York: Knopf, 1957
SOMETHING ABOUT A SOLDIER. New York: Macmillan, 1957
WAKE UP, STUPID. New York: Knopf, 1959

L[ESLIE] P[OLES] HARTLEY (1895-   )

SIMONETTA PERKINS. London: Putnam, 1925
THE SHRIMP AND THE ANEMONE.[1] London: Putnam, 1944. Garden City: Doubleday, Doran, 1945, under the title THE WEST WINDOW
THE SIXTH HEAVEN.[1] London: Putnam, 1946
EUSTACE AND HILDA.[1] London: Putnam, 1947. *James Tait Black Memorial Prize, 1948*
THE BOAT. London: Putnam, 1949
MY FELLOW DEVILS. London: Barrie, 1951
THE GO-BETWEEN. London: Hamilton, 1953. *Heinemann Award, 1954*
A PERFECT WOMAN. London: Hamilton, 1955
THE HIRELING. London: Hamilton, 1957
FACIAL JUSTICE. London: Hamilton, 1960
THE BRICKFIELD. London: Hamilton, 1964
THE BETRAYAL. London: Hamilton, 1966
[1]A trilogy: EUSTACE AND HILDA, London: Putnam, 1958

JOHN [CLENDENNIN BURNE] HAWKES [JR.] (1925-   )

THE CANNIBAL. New York: New Directions, 1949
THE BEETLE LEG. New York: New Directions, 1951
THE LIME TWIG. Norfolk, Conn.: New Directions, 1961
SECOND SKIN. Norfolk, Conn.: New Directions, 1964

ALFRED HAYES (1911-   )

ALL THY CONQUESTS. New York: Howell, Soskin, 1946
SHADOW OF HEAVEN. New York: Howell, Soskin, 1947
THE GIRL ON THE VIA FLAMINIA. New York: Harper, 1949
IN LOVE. New York: Harper, 1953
MY FACE FOR THE WORLD TO SEE. New York: Harper, 1958

JOHN [EDGAR CAULWELL] HEARNE (1925-   )

VOICES UNDER THE WINDOW. London: Faber & Faber, 1955.
John Llewelyn Rhys Memorial Prize, 1956
STRANGER AT THE GATE. London: Faber & Faber, 1956
THE FACES OF LOVE. London: Faber & Faber, 1957. Boston:
Little, Brown, 1958, under the title THE EYE OF THE STORM
THE AUTUMN EQUINOX. London: Faber & Faber, 1959. New
York: Vanguard, 1961, under the title AUTUMN EQUINOX
LAND OF THE LIVING. London: Faber & Faber, 1961

THOMAS [ORLO] HEGGEN (1919-1949)

MISTER ROBERTS. Boston: Houghton Mifflin, 1946

JOSEPH HELLER (1923-   )

CATCH-22. New York: Simon & Schuster, 1961

ERNEST [MILLER] HEMINGWAY (1899-1961)

Award of Merit Medal for the Novel, American Academy of Arts
and Letters, 1954. Nobel Prize for Literature, 1954
THE TORRENTS OF SPRING. New York: Scribner, 1926
THE SUN ALSO RISES. New York: Scribner, 1926. London: Cape,
1927, under the title FIESTA
A FAREWELL TO ARMS. New York: Scribner, 1929
TO HAVE AND HAVE NOT. New York: Scribner, 1937
FOR WHOM THE BELL TOLLS. New York: Scribner, 1940
ACROSS THE RIVER AND INTO THE TREES. New York:
Scribner, 1950
THE OLD MAN AND THE SEA. New York: Scribner, 1952.
Pulitzer Prize, 1953

ROBERT [DAVID QUIXANO] HENRIQUES (1905-   )

NO ARMS, NO ARMOUR. London: Nicholson & Watson, 1939

CAPTAIN SMITH AND COMPANY. London: Heinemann, 1943.
New York: Farrar & Rinehart, 1943, under the title THE VOICE
OF THE TRUMPET
THE JOURNEY HOME. London: Heinemann, 1944. New York:
Viking, 1945, under the title HOME FIRES BURNING
THROUGH THE VALLEY. London: Collins, 1950. New York:
Viking, 1950, under the title TOO LITTLE LOVE. *James Tait
Black Memorial Prize, 1951*
A STRANGER HERE. London: Collins, 1953
RED OVER GREEN. London: Collins, 1956

[JOHN] RAYNER HEPPENSTALL (1911-   )

THE BLAZE OF NOON. London: Secker & Warburg, 1939
SATURNINE. London: Secker & Warburg, 1943. Reissued as THE
GREATER INFORTUNE, London: Owen, 1960
THE LESSER INFORTUNE. London: Cape, 1953
THE CONNECTING DOOR. London: Barrie & Rockliff, 1962
THE WOODSHED. London: Barrie & Rockliff, 1962

JOSEPH HERGESHEIMER (1880-1954)

THE LAY ANTHONY. New York: Kennerley, 1914
MOUNTAIN BLOOD. New York: Kennerley, 1915
THE THREE BLACK PENNYS. New York: Knopf, 1917
JAVA HEAD. New York: Knopf, 1919
LINDA CONDON. New York: Knopf, 1919
CYTHEREA. New York: Knopf, 1922
THE BRIGHT SHAWL. New York: Knopf, 1922
BALISAND. New York: Knopf, 1924
TAMPICO. New York: Knopf, 1926
THE PARTY DRESS. New York: Knopf, 1930
THE LIMESTONE TREE. New York: Knopf, 1931
THE FOOLSCAP ROSE. New York: Knopf, 1934

JAMES LEO HERLIHY (1927-   )

ALL FALL DOWN. New York: Dutton, 1960
MIDNIGHT COWBOY. New York: Simon & Schuster, 1965

ROBERT HERRICK (1868-1938)

THE MAN WHO WINS. New York: Scribner, 1897
THE GOSPEL OF FREEDOM. New York: Macmillan, 1898
THE WEB OF LIFE. New York: Macmillan, 1900
THE REAL WORLD. New York: Macmillan, 1901

THEIR CHILD. New York: Macmillan, 1903
THE COMMON LOT. New York: Macmillan, 1904
THE MEMOIRS OF AN AMERICAN CITIZEN. New York: Macmillan, 1905
THE MASTER OF THE INN. New York: Scribner, 1908
TOGETHER. New York: Macmillan, 1908
A LIFE FOR A LIFE. New York: Macmillan, 1910
THE HEALER. New York: Macmillan, 1911
HIS GREAT ADVENTURE. New York: Macmillan, 1913
ONE WOMAN'S LIFE. New York: Macmillan, 1913
CLARK'S FIELD. Boston: Houghton Mifflin, 1914
THE CONSCRIPT MOTHER. New York: Scribner, 1916
HOMELY LILLA. New York: Harcourt, Brace, 1923
WASTE. New York: Harcourt, Brace, 1924
CHIMES. New York: Macmillan, 1926
THE END OF DESIRE. New York: Farrar & Rinehart, 1932
SOMETIME. New York: Farrar & Rinehart, 1933

JOHN [RICHARD] HERSEY (1914-   )

A BELL FOR ADANO. New York: Knopf, 1944. *Pulitzer Prize, 1945*
THE WALL. New York: Knopf, 1950
THE MARMOT DRIVE. New York: Knopf, 1953
A SINGLE PEBBLE. New York: Knopf, 1956
THE WAR LOVER. New York: Knopf, 1959
THE CHILD BUYER. New York: Knopf, 1960
WHITE LOTUS. New York: 1965
TOO FAR TO WALK. New York: Knopf, 1966

MAURICE [HENRY] HEWLETT (1861-1923)

THE FOREST LOVERS. London: Macmillan, 1898
RICHARD YEA-AND-NAY. London: Macmillan, 1900
THE QUEEN'S QUAIR. London: Macmillan, 1904
THE FOOL ERRANT. London: Heinemann, 1905
THE STOOPING LADY. London: Macmillan, 1907
THE SPANISH JADE. London: Cassell, 1908
HALFWAY HOUSE.[1] London: Chapman & Hall, 1908
OPEN COUNTRY.[1] London: Macmillan, 1909
REST HARROW.[1] London: Macmillan, 1910
BRAZENHEAD THE GREAT. London: Smith, Elder, 1911
THE SONG OF RENNY. London: Macmillan, 1911
MRS. LANCELOT. London: Macmillan, 1912
BENDISH. London: Macmillan, 1913
A LOVER'S TALE. London: Ward, Lock, 1915

THE LITTLE ILIAD. London: Heinemann, 1915
FREY AND HIS WIFE. London: Ward, Lock, 1916
LOVE AND LUCY. London: Macmillan, 1916
THORGILS OF TREADHOLT. London: Ward, Lock, 1917. New
    York: Dodd, Mead, 1917, under the title THORGILS
GUDRID THE FAIR. London: Constable, 1918
THE OUTLAW. London: Constable, 1919
THE LIGHT HEART. London: Chapman & Hall, 1920
MAINWARING. New York: Dodd, Mead, 1920. London: Collins,
    1921

[1]A trilogy

DuBOSE HEYWARD (1885-1940)

PORGY. New York: Doran, 1925
ANGEL. New York: Doran, 1926
MAMBA'S DAUGHTERS. Garden City: Doubleday, Doran, 1929
PETER ASHLEY. New York: Farrar & Rinehart, 1932
LOST MORNING. New York: Farrar & Rinehart, 1936
STAR SPANGLED VIRGIN. New York: Farrar & Rinehart, 1939

JAMES HILTON (1900-1954)

CATHERINE HERSELF. London: Unwin, 1920
STORM PASSAGE. London: Unwin, 1922
THE PASSIONATE YEAR. London: Butterworth, 1923
THE DAWN OF RECKONING. London: Butterworth, 1925. New
    York: King, 1932, under the title RAGE IN HEAVEN
THE MEADOWS OF THE MOON. London: Butterworth, 1926
TERRY. London: Butterworth, 1927
THE SILVER FLAME. London: Butterworth, 1928
AND NOW GOOD-BYE. London: Benn, 1931
MURDER AT SCHOOL (by "Glen Trevor"). London: Benn, 1931.
    New York: Harper, 1935, under the title WAS IT MURDER?
CONTANGO. London: Benn, 1932. New York: Morrow, 1932, under
    the title ILL WIND
KNIGHT WITHOUT ARMOUR. London: Benn, 1933. New York:
    Morrow, 1934, under the title WITHOUT ARMOR
LOST HORIZON. London: Macmillan, 1933. *Hawthornden Prize,
    1934*
GOOD-BYE, MR. CHIPS. London: Hodder & Stoughton, 1934
WE ARE NOT ALONE. London: Macmillan, 1937
RANDOM HARVEST. London: Macmillan, 1941
THE STORY OF DR. WASSELL. Boston: Atlantic-Little, Brown,
    1943. London: Macmillan, 1944

SO WELL REMEMBERED. Boston: Atlantic-Little, Brown, 1945.
London: Macmillan, 1947
NOTHING SO STRANGE. Boston: Atlantic-Little, Brown, 1947.
London: Macmillan, 1948
MORNING JOURNEY. London: Macmillan, 1951
TIME AND TIME AGAIN. London: Macmillan, 1953

THOMAS HINDE, i.e. Sir THOMAS WILLES CHITTY (1926-   )

MR. NICHOLAS. London: MacGibbon & Kee, 1952
HAPPY AS LARRY. London: MacGibbon & Kee, 1957
FOR THE GOOD OF THE COMPANY. London: Hutchinson, 1961
A PLACE LIKE HOME. London: Hodder & Stoughton, 1962
THE CAGE. London: Hodder & Stoughton, 1962
NINETY DOUBLE MARTINIS. London: Hodder & Stoughton, 1963
THE DAY THE CALL CAME. London: Hodder & Stoughton, 1964
THE VILLAGE. London: Hodder & Stoughton, 1966

H[ARRY] S[UMMERFIELD] HOFF: See WILLIAM COOPER

CONSTANCE HOLME (18 -1955)

CRUMP FOLK GOING HOME. London: Mills & Boon, 1913
THE LONELY PLOUGH. London: Mills & Boon, 1914
THE OLD ROAD FROM SPAIN. London: Mills & Boon, 1916
BEAUTIFUL END. London: Mills & Boon, 1918
THE SPLENDID FAIRING. London: Mills & Boon, 1919. *Femina-Vie Heureuse Prize, 1921*
THE TRUMPET IN THE DUST. London: Mills & Boon, 1921
THE THINGS WHICH BELONG. London: Mills & Boon, 1925
HE-WHO-CAME? London: Chapman & Hall, 1930

WINIFRED HOLTBY (1898-1935)

ANDERBY WOLD. London: Lane, 1923
THE CROWDED STREET. London: Lane, 1924
THE LAND OF GREEN GINGER. London: Cape, 1927
POOR CAROLINE. London: Cape, 1931
MANDOA, MANDOA! London: Collins, 1933
THE ASTONISHING ISLAND. London: Dickson, 1933
SOUTH RIDING. London: Collins, 1936. *James Tait Black Memorial Prize, 1937*

STEPHEN HUDSON, i.e. SYDNEY SCHIFF (1868-1944)

CONCESSIONS. London: Lane, 1913
RICHARD KURT.[1] London: Secker, 1919
ELINOR COLHOUSE.[1] London: Secker, 1921
PRINCE HEMPSEED.[1] London: Secker, 1923
TONY. London: Constable, 1924
MYRTLE.[1] London: Constable, 1925
RICHARD, MYRTLE AND I. London: Constable, 1926
A TRUE STORY.[1] London: Constable, 1930
THE OTHER SIDE.[1] London: Cresset, 1937

[1]A series; collected in one volume as A TRUE STORY, London: Dent, 1965
Note: Only the first novel was published under the name Sydney Schiff

FORD HERMANN MADOX HUEFFER: See FORD MADOX FORD

RICHARD [ARTHUR WARREN] HUGHES (1900-   )

A HIGH WIND IN JAMAICA. London: Chatto & Windus, 1929.
    New York: Harper, 1929, under the title THE INNOCENT
    VOYAGE. *Femina-Vie Heureuse Prize, 1931*
IN HAZARD. London: Chatto & Windus, 1938
THE FOX IN THE ATTIC.[1] London: Chatto & Windus, 1961

[1]Vol. I of THE HUMAN PREDICAMENT

H[AROLD] L[OUIS] HUMES, JR. (1926-   )

THE UNDERGROUND CITY. New York: Random House, 1958
MEN DIE. New York: Random House, 1959

WILLIAM HUMPHREY (1924-   )

HOME FROM THE HILL. New York: Knopf, 1958
THE ORDWAYS. New York: Knopf, 1965

EMYR [OWEN] HUMPHREYS (1919-   )

THE LITTLE KINGDOM. London: Eyre & Spottiswoode, 1946
THE VOICE OF A STRANGER. London: Eyre & Spottiswoode,
    1949
A CHANGE OF HEART. London: Eyre & Spottiswoode, 1951
HEAR AND FORGIVE. London: Gollancz, 1952. *Somerset Maugham
    Award, 1953*
A MAN'S ESTATE. London: Eyre & Spottiswoode, 1955

THE ITALIAN WIFE. London: Eyre & Spottiswoode, 1957
A TOY EPIC. London: Eyre & Spottiswoode, 1958. *Hawthornden Prize, 1959*
THE GIFT. London: Eyre & Spottiswoode, 1963
OUTSIDE THE HOUSE OF BAAL. London: Eyre & Spottiswoode, 1965

JIM HUNTER (1939-   )

THE SUN IN THE MORNING. London: Faber & Faber, 1961. *Authors' Club First Novel Award, 1962*
SALLY CRAY. London: Faber & Faber, 1963
EARTH AND STONE. London: Faber & Faber, 1963. New York: Pantheon, 1964, under the title A PLACE OF STONE
THE FLAME. London: Faber & Faber, 1966

R[AY] C[ORYTON] HUTCHINSON (1907-   )

THOU HAST A DEVIL. London: Benn, 1930
THE ANSWERING GLORY. London: Cassell, 1932
THE UNFORGOTTEN PRISONER. London: Cassell, 1933
ONE LIGHT BURNING. London: Cassell, 1935
SHINING SCABBARD. London: Cassell, 1936
TESTAMENT. London: Cassell, 1938
THE FIRE AND THE WOOD. London: Cassell, 1940
INTERIM. London: Cassell, 1945
ELEPHANT AND CASTLE. London: Cassell, 1949
RECOLLECTION OF A JOURNEY. London: Cassell, 1952. New York: Rinehart, 1952, under the title JOURNEY WITH STRANGERS
THE STEPMOTHER. London: Cassell, 1955
MARCH THE NINTH. London: Bles, 1957
IMAGE OF MY FATHER. London: Bles, 1961. New York: Harper, 1961, under the title THE INHERITOR
A CHILD POSSESSED. London: Bles, 1964. *W. H. Smith & Son Literary Award, 1966*

ALDOUS [LEONARD] HUXLEY, C.Litt. (1894-1963)

Award of Merit Medal for the Novel, American Academy of Arts and Letters, 1959
CROME YELLOW. London: Chatto & Windus, 1921
ANTIC HAY. London: Chatto & Windus, 1923
THOSE BARREN LEAVES. London: Chatto & Windus, 1925

POINT COUNTER POINT. London: Chatto & Windus, 1928
BRAVE NEW WORLD. London: Chatto & Windus, 1932
EYELESS IN GAZA. London: Chatto & Windus, 1936
AFTER MANY A SUMMER. London: Chatto & Windus, 1939. New
York: Harper, 1939, under the title AFTER MANY A SUMMER
DIES THE SWAN. *James Tait Black Memorial Prize, 1940*
TIME MUST HAVE A STOP. New York: Harper, 1944. London:
Chatto & Windus, 1945
APE AND ESSENCE. New York: Harper, 1948. London: Chatto &
Windus, 1949
THE GENIUS AND THE GODDESS. London: Chatto & Windus,
1955
ISLAND. London: Chatto & Windus, 1962

CHRISTOPHER [WILLIAM BRADSHAW] ISHERWOOD (1904-   )

ALL THE CONSPIRATORS. London: Cape, 1928
THE MEMORIAL. London: Hogarth, 1932
MR. NORRIS CHANGES TRAINS.[1] London: Hogarth, 1935. New
York: Morrow, 1935, under the title THE LAST OF MR.
NORRIS
GOODBYE TO BERLIN.[1] London: Hogarth, 1939
PRATER VIOLET. New York: Random House, 1945. London:
Methuen, 1946
THE WORLD IN THE EVENING. London: Methuen, 1954
DOWN THERE ON A VISIT. London: Methuen, 1962
A SINGLE MAN. London: Methuen, 1964
[1]THE BERLIN STORIES, New York: Laughlin [New Directions], 1946

SHIRLEY JACKSON (1919-1965)

THE ROAD THROUGH THE WALL. New York: Farrar, Straus,
1948
HANGSAMAN. New York: Farrar, Straus & Young, 1951
THE BIRD'S NEST. New York: Farrar, Straus & Young, 1954
THE SUNDIAL. New York: Farrar, Straus & Cudahy, 1958
THE HAUNTING OF HILL HOUSE. New York: Viking, 1959
WE HAVE ALWAYS LIVED IN THE CASTLE. New York: Viking,
1962

DAN JACOBSON (1929-   )

THE TRAP. London: Weidenfeld & Nicolson, 1955
A DANCE IN THE SUN. London: Weidenfeld & Nicolson, 1956

THE PRICE OF DIAMONDS. London: Weidenfeld & Nicolson, 1957
THE EVIDENCE OF LOVE. London: Weidenfeld & Nicolson, 1960.
    Boston: Atlantic-Little, Brown, 1960, under the title EVIDENCE OF LOVE
THE BEGINNERS. London: Weidenfeld & Nicolson, 1966

[MARGARET] STORM JAMESON (1897-   )

THE POT BOILS. London: Constable, 1919
THE HAPPY HIGHWAYS. London: Heinemann, 1920
THE CLASH. London: Heinemann, 1922
LADY SUSAN AND LIFE. London: Chapman & Dodd, 1923
THE PITIFUL WIFE. London: Constable, 1923
THREE KINGDOMS. London: Constable, 1926
THE LOVELY SHIP.[1] London: Heinemann, 1927
FAREWELL TO YOUTH. London: Heinemann, 1928
THE VOYAGE HOME.[1] London: Heinemann, 1930
A RICHER DUST.[1] London: Heinemann, 1931
THE SINGLE HEART.[2] London: Benn, 1932
THAT WAS YESTERDAY. London: Heinemann, 1932
A DAY OFF.[2] London: Nicholson & Watson, 1933
COMPANY PARADE.[3] London: Cassell, 1934
LOVE IN WINTER.[3] London: Cassell, 1935
NONE TURN BACK.[3] London: Cassell, 1936
IN THE SECOND YEAR. London: Cassell, 1936
DELICATE MONSTER.[2] London: Nicholson & Watson, 1937
THE MOON IS MAKING. London: Cassell, 1937
HERE COMES A CANDLE. London: Cassell, 1938
FAREWELL NIGHT; WELCOME DAY. London: Cassell, 1939.
    New York: Macmillan, 1939, under the title THE CAPTAIN'S WIFE
EUROPE TO LET. London: Macmillan, 1940
COUSIN HONORÉ. London: Cassell, 1940
THE FORT. London: Cassell, 1941
THEN WE SHALL HEAR SINGING. London: Cassell, 1942
CLOUDLESS MAY. London: Macmillan, 1943
THE JOURNAL OF MARY HERVEY RUSSELL. London: Macmillan, 1945
THE OTHER SIDE. London: Macmillan, 1946
BEFORE THE CROSSING. London: Macmillan, 1947
THE BLACK LAUREL. London: Macmillan, 1948
THE MOMENT OF TRUTH. London: Macmillan, 1949
THE GREEN MAN. London: Macmillan, 1952

THE HIDDEN RIVER. London: Macmillan, 1955
THE INTRUDER. London: Macmillan, 1956
A CUP OF TEA FOR MR. THORGILL. London: Macmillan, 1957
A ULYSSES TOO MANY. London: Macmillan, 1958. New York:
    Harper, 1958, under the title ONE ULYSSES TOO MANY
LAST SCORE. London: Macmillan, 1961
THE ROAD FROM THE MONUMENT. London: Macmillan, 1962
A MONTH SOON GOES. London: Macmillan, 1963
THE ARISTIDE CASE. London: Macmillan, 1964. New York:
    Harper & Row, 1964, under the title THE BLIND HEART
THE EARLY LIFE OF STEPHEN HIND. London: Macmillan, 1966
[1]A trilogy: THE TRIUMPH OF TIME, London: Heinemann, 1932
[2]Collected as WOMEN AGAINST MEN, New York: Knopf, 1933
[3]A trilogy: THE MIRROR IN DARKNESS

ELIZABETH JENKINS (1907-   )

VIRGINIA WATER. London: Gollancz, 1929
THE WINTERS. London: Gollancz, 1931
PORTRAIT OF AN ACTOR. London: Gollancz, 1933
HARRIET. London: Gollancz, 1934. *Femina-Vie Heureuse Prize,
    1935*
DOUBTFUL JOY. London: Gollancz, 1935
THE PHOENIX' NEST. London: Gollancz, 1936
ROBERT AND HELEN. London: Gollancz, 1944
YOUNG ENTHUSIASTS. London: Gollancz, 1947
THE TORTOISE AND THE HARE. London: Gollancz, 1954
BRIGHTNESS. London: Gollancz, 1963

R[UTH] PRAWER JHABVALA (1927-   )

TO WHOM SHE WILL. London: Allen & Unwin, 1955. New York:
    Norton, 1956, under the title AMRITA
THE NATURE OF PASSION. London: Allen & Unwin, 1956
ESMOND IN INDIA. London: Allen & Unwin, 1958
THE HOUSEHOLDER. London: Murray, 1960
GET READY FOR BATTLE. London: Murray, 1962
A BACKWARD PLACE. London: Murray, 1965

JOSEPHINE WINSLOW JOHNSON (1910-   )

NOW IN NOVEMBER. New York: Simon & Schuster, 1934. *Pulitzer
    Prize, 1935*
JORDANSTOWN. New York: Simon & Schuster, 1937
WILDWOOD. New York: Harper, 1946
THE DARK TRAVELER. New York: Simon & Schuster, 1963

PAMELA HANSFORD JOHNSON (1912-   )
THIS BED THY CENTRE. London: Chapman & Hall, 1935
BLESSED ABOVE WOMEN. London: Chapman & Hall, 1936
HERE TO-DAY. London: Chapman & Hall, 1937
WORLD'S END. London: Chapman & Hall, 1937
THE MONUMENT. London: Chapman & Hall, 1938
GIRDLE OF VENUS. London: Chapman & Hall, 1939
TOO DEAR FOR MY POSSESSING.[1] London: Collins, 1940
THE FAMILY PATTERN. London: Collins, 1942
WINTER QUARTERS. London: Collins, 1943
THE TROJAN BROTHERS. London: Joseph, 1944
AN AVENUE OF STONE.[1] London: Joseph, 1947
A SUMMER TO DECIDE.[1] London: Joseph, 1948
THE PHILISTINES. London: Joseph, 1949
CATHERINE CARTER. London: Macmillan, 1952
AN IMPOSSIBLE MARRIAGE. London: Macmillan, 1954
THE LAST RESORT. London: Macmillan, 1956. New York: Harcourt, Brace, 1957, under the title THE SEA AND THE WEDDING
THE UNSPEAKABLE SKIPTON. London: Macmillan, 1959
THE HUMBLER CREATION. London: Macmillan, 1959
AN ERROR OF JUDGEMENT. London: Macmillan, 1962
NIGHT AND SILENCE WHO IS HERE? London: Macmillan, 1963
CORK STREET, NEXT TO THE HATTER'S. London: Macmillan, 1965
[1]A trilogy

DAVID [MICHAEL] JONES (1895-   )
IN PARENTHESIS. London: Faber & Faber, 1937. *Hawthornden Prize, 1938*

JAMES JONES (1921-   )
FROM HERE TO ETERNITY. New York: Scribner, 1951. *National Book Award, 1952*
SOME CAME RUNNING. New York: Scribner, 1957
THE PISTOL. New York: Scribner, 1959
THE THIN RED LINE. New York: Scribner, 1962

MADISON [PERCY] JONES [JR.] (1925-   )
THE INNOCENT. New York: Harcourt, Brace, 1957
FOREST OF THE NIGHT. New York: Harcourt, Brace, 1960
A BURIED LAND. New York: Viking, 1963

JAMES [AUGUSTINE ALOYSIUS] JOYCE (1882-1941)

A PORTRAIT OF THE ARTIST AS A YOUNG MAN.[1] New York: Huebsch, 1916. London: Egoist, 1917

ULYSSES. Paris: Shakespeare, 1922. London: Egoist, 1922

FINNEGANS WAKE. London: Faber & Faber, 1939

[1]A part of the first draft of this work has been published as STEPHEN HERO, Norfolk, Conn.: New Directions, 1944 (with additions, 1955); London: Cape, 1944 (with additions, 1956).

MacKINLAY KANTOR (1904-   )

DIVERSEY. New York: Coward-McCann, 1928

EL GOES SOUTH. New York: Coward-McCann, 1930

THE JAYBIRD. New York: Coward-McCann, 1932

LONG REMEMBER. New York: Coward-McCann, 1934

THE VOICE OF BUGLE ANN. New York: Coward-McCann, 1935

AROUSE AND BEWARE. New York: Coward-McCann, 1936

THE ROMANCE OF ROSY RIDGE. New York: Coward-McCann, 1937

THE NOISE OF THEIR WINGS. New York: Coward-McCann, 1938

VALEDICTORY. New York: Coward-McCann, 1939

CUBA LIBRE. New York: Coward-McCann, 1940

GENTLE ANNIE. New York: Coward-McCann, 1942

HAPPY LAND. New York: Coward-McCann, 1943

MIDNIGHT LACE. New York: Random House, 1948

WICKED WATER. New York: Random House, 1949

THE GOOD FAMILY. New York: Coward-McCann, 1949

SIGNAL THIRTY-TWO. New York: Random House, 1950

ONE WILD OAT. New York: Fawcett, 1950

DON'T TOUCH ME. New York: Random House, 1951

THE DAUGHTER OF BUGLE ANN. New York: Random House, 1953

GOD AND MY COUNTRY. Cleveland: World, 1954

ANDERSONVILLE. Cleveland: World, 1955. *Pulitzer Prize, 1956*

THE WORK OF SAINT FRANCIS. Cleveland: World, 1958. London: Allen, 1959, under the title THE UNSEEN WITNESS

SPIRIT LAKE. Cleveland: World, 1961

SHEILA KAYE-SMITH (1887-1956)

THE TRAMPING METHODIST. London: Bell, 1908

STARBRACE. London: Bell, 1909

SPELL LAND. London: Bell, 1910

ISLE OF THORNS. London: Constable, 1913
THREE AGAINST THE WORLD. London: Chapman & Hall, 1914.
　　Philadelphia: Lippincott, 1914, under the title THE THREE
　　FURLONGERS
SUSSEX GORSE. London: Nisbet, 1916
THE CHALLENGE TO SIRIUS. London: Nisbet, 1917
LITTLE ENGLAND. London: Nisbet, 1918. New York: Doran,
　　1919, under the title THE FOUR ROADS
TAMARISK TOWN. London: Cassell, 1919
GREEN APPLE HARVEST. London: Cassell, 1920
JOANNA GODDEN. London: Cassell, 1921
THE END OF THE HOUSE OF ALARD. London: Cassell, 1923
THE GEORGE AND THE CROWN. London: Cassell, 1925
IRON AND SMOKE. London: Cassell, 1928
THE VILLAGE DOCTOR. London: Cassell, 1929
SHEPHERDS IN SACKCLOTH. London: Cassell, 1930
THE HISTORY OF SUSAN SPRAY, THE FEMALE PREACHER.
　　London: Cassell, 1931. New York: Harper, 1931, under the
　　title SUSAN SPRAY
THE CHILDREN'S SUMMER. London: Cassell, 1932. New York:
　　Harper, 1932, under the title SUMMER HOLIDAY
THE PLOUGHMAN'S PROGRESS. London: Cassell, 1933. New
　　York: Harper, 1933, under the title GIPSY WAGGON
SUPERSTITION CORNER. London: Cassell, 1934
GALLYBIRD. London: Cassell, 1934
SELINA IS OLDER. London: Cassell, 1935. New York: Harper,
　　1935, under the title SELINA
ROSE DEEPROSE. London: Cassell, 1936
THE VALIANT WOMAN. New York: Harper, 1938. London: Cas-
　　sell, 1939
EMBER LANE. London: Cassell, 1940
THE HIDDEN SON. London: Cassell, 1941. New York: Harper,
　　1942, under the title THE SECRET SON
TAMBOURINE, TRUMPET AND DRUM. London: Cassell, 1943
THE LARDNERS AND THE LAURELWOODS. New York: Harper,
　　1947. London: Cassell, 1948
THE TREASURES OF THE SNOW. London: Cassell, 1950. New
　　York: Harper, 1949, under the title THE HAPPY TREE
MRS. GAILEY. London: Cassell, 1951
THE VIEW FROM THE PARSONAGE. London: Cassell, 1954

**JOSEPH KELL: See [JOHN] ANTHONY
BURGESS [WILSON]**

WILLIAM MELVIN KELLEY (1937-   )
A DIFFERENT DRUMMER. Garden City: Doubleday, 1962.
  Rosenthal Award, 1963
A DROP OF PATIENCE. Garden City: Doubleday, 1965

JAMES KENNAWAY (1928-   )
TUNES OF GLORY. London: Putnam, 1956
HOUSEHOLD GHOSTS. London: Longmans, 1961
THE MIND BENDERS. London: Longmans, 1963
THE BELLS OF SHOREDITCH. London: Longmans, 1963

MARGARET [MOORE] KENNEDY (1896-   )
THE LADIES OF LYNDON. London: Heinemann, 1923
THE CONSTANT NYMPH. London: Heinemann, 1924
A LONG WEEK-END. London: Heinemann, 1927
RED SKY AT MORNING. London: Heinemann, 1927
THE FOOL OF THE FAMILY. London: Heinemann, 1930
RETURN I DARE NOT. London: Heinemann, 1931
A LONG TIME AGO. London: Heinemann, 1932
TOGETHER AND APART. London: Cassell, 1936
THE MIDAS TOUCH. London: Cassell, 1938
THE FEAST. London: Cassell, 1950
LUCY CARMICHAEL. London: Macmillan, 1951
TROY CHIMNEYS. New York: Rinehart, 1952. London: Mac-
    millan, 1953. *James Tait Black Memorial Prize, 1954*
THE ORACLES. London: Macmillan, 1955. New York: Rinehart,
    1955, under the title ACT OF GOD
THE HEROES OF CLONE. London: Macmillan, 1957. New York:
    Rinehart, 1957, under the title THE WILD SWAN
A NIGHT IN COLD HARBOUR. London: Macmillan, 1960
THE FORGOTTEN SMILE. London: Macmillan, 1961
NOT IN THE CALENDAR. London: Macmillan, 1964

[JEAN-LOUIS] JACK KEROUAC (1922-   )
THE TOWN AND THE CITY. New York: Harcourt, Brace, 1950
ON THE ROAD. New York: Viking, 1957
THE SUBTERRANEANS. New York: Grove, 1958
THE DHARMA BUMS. New York: Viking, 1958
DOCTOR SAX. New York: Grove, 1959
MAGGIE CASSIDY. New York: Avon, 1959
VISIONS OF CODY. Norfolk, Conn.: New Directions, 1959
TRISTESSA. New York: Avon, 1960

BIG SUR. New York: Farrar, Straus, 1962
VISIONS OF GERARD. New York: Farrar, Straus, 1963
DESOLATION ANGELS. New York: Coward-McCann, 1965

FRANCIS [HENRY] KING (1923-   )
TO THE DARK TOWER. London: Home & Van Thal, 1946
NEVER AGAIN. London: Home & Van Thal, 1947
AN AIR THAT KILLS. London: Home & Van Thal, 1948
THE DIVIDING STREAM. London: Longmans, 1951. *Somerset Maugham Award, 1952*
THE DARK GLASSES. London: Longmans, 1954
THE FIREWALKERS (by "Frank Cauldwell"). London: Murray, 1956
THE WIDOW. London: Longmans, 1957
THE MAN ON THE ROCK. London: Longmans, 1957
THE CUSTOM HOUSE. London: Longmans, 1961
THE LAST OF THE PLEASURE GARDENS. London: Longmans, 1965

JOHN KNOWLES (1926-   )
A SEPARATE PEACE. New York: Macmillan, 1960. *Rosenthal Award, 1961. William Faulkner Foundation Award, 1961*
MORNING IN ANTIBES. New York: Macmillan, 1962
INDIAN SUMMER. New York: Random House, 1966

ARTHUR KOESTLER (1905-   )
ARRIVAL AND DEPARTURE. London: Cape, 1943
THIEVES IN THE NIGHT. London: Macmillan, 1946
THE AGE OF LONGING. London: Collins, 1951
Translated from the German:
THE GLADIATORS. London: Cape, 1939
DARKNESS AT NOON. London: Cape, 1940

BERNARD KOPS (1926-   )
AWAKE FOR MOURNING. London: MacGibbon & Kee, 1958
YES FROM NO MAN'S LAND. London: MacGibbon & Kee, 1965
THE DISSENT OF DOMINICK SHAPIRO. London: MacGibbon & Kee, 1966

OLIVER [HAZARD PERRY] LA FARGE (1901-1963)
LAUGHING BOY. Boston: Houghton Mifflin, 1929. *Pulitzer Prize, 1930*

SPARKS FLY UPWARD. Boston: Houghton Mifflin, 1931
LONG PENNANT. Boston: Houghton Mifflin, 1933
THE ENEMY GODS. Boston: Houghton Mifflin, 1937
THE COPPER POT. Boston: Houghton Mifflin, 1942

GEORGE LAMMING (1927-)

IN THE CASTLE OF MY SKIN. London: Joseph, 1953. *Somerset Maugham Award, 1957*
THE EMIGRANTS. London: Joseph, 1954
OF AGE AND INNOCENCE. London: Joseph, 1958
SEASON OF ADVENTURE. London: Joseph, 1960

MARGARET LANE (1907-)

FAITH, HOPE, NO CHARITY. London: Heinemann, 1935. *Femina-Vie Heureuse Prize, 1937*
AT LAST THE ISLAND. London: Heinemann, 1937
WALK INTO MY PARLOUR. London: Heinemann, 1941
WHERE HELEN LIES. London: Heinemann, 1944
A NIGHT AT SEA. London: Hamilton, 1964
A SMELL OF BURNING. London: Hamilton, 1965

PHILIP [ARTHUR] LARKIN (1922-)

JILL. London: Fortune, 1946
A GIRL IN WINTER. London: Faber & Faber, 1947

MARY LAVIN (1912-)

THE HOUSE IN CLEWE STREET. London: Joseph, 1945
MARY O'GRADY. London: Joseph, 1950

D[AVID] H[ERBERT] LAWRENCE (1885-1930)

THE WHITE PEACOCK. London: Heinemann, 1911
THE TRESPASSER. London: Duckworth, 1912
SONS AND LOVERS. London: Duckworth, 1913
THE RAINBOW. London: Methuen, 1915
WOMEN IN LOVE. New York: Privately printed [Seltzer], 1920. London: Secker, 1921
THE LOST GIRL. London: Secker, 1920. *James Tait Black Memorial Prize, 1921*
AARON'S ROD. London: Secker, 1922
KANGAROO. London: Secker, 1923
THE BOY IN THE BUSH (in collaboration with M. L. Skinner). London: Secker, 1924

THE PLUMED SERPENT. London: Secker, 1926
LADY CHATTERLEY'S LOVER.[1] Florence: Privately printed
[Giuntina], 1928. London: Secker, 1932 (*expurgated*).
New York: Grove, 1959 (*unexpurgated*). Harmondsworth, Middle-
sex: Penguin Books, 1960 (*unexpurgated*)
THE VIRGIN AND THE GIPSY. Florence: Orioli, 1930. London:
Secker, 1930
MR. NOON (*fragment*), in a MODERN LOVER. London: Secker,
1934

[1]The first MS version of this work was published as THE FIRST LADY
CHATTERLEY, New York: Dial, 1944; the second MS version was
published in LE TRE "LADY CHATTERLEY," Milan: Mondadori, 1954.

JOHN LE CARRÉ, i.e DAVID JOHN MOORE CORNWELL (1931-   )
CALL FOR THE DEAD.[1] London: Gollancz, 1960
A MURDER OF QUALITY.[1] London: Gollancz, 1962
THE SPY WHO CAME IN FROM THE COLD. London: Gollancz,
1963. *Somerset Maugham Award, 1964*
THE LOOKING-GLASS WAR. London: Heinemann, 1965
[1]Collected as THE INCONGRUOUS SPY, New York: Walker, 1964

ANDREW LEE: See LOUIS [STANTON] AUCHINCLOSS

[NELLE] HARPER LEE (1926-   )
TO KILL A MOCKINGBIRD. Philadelphia: Lippincott, 1960.
Pulitzer Prize, 1961

ROSAMOND [NINA] LEHMANN (1904-   )
DUSTY ANSWER. London: Chatto & Windus, 1927
A NOTE IN MUSIC. London: Chatto & Windus, 1930
INVITATION TO THE WALTZ. London: Chatto & Windus, 1932
THE WEATHER IN THE STREETS. London: Collins, 1936
THE BALLAD AND THE SOURCE. London: Collins, 1944
THE ECHOING GROVE. London: Collins, 1953

DORIS [MAY] LESSING (1919-   )
THE GRASS IS SINGING. London: Joseph, 1950
MARTHA QUEST.[1] London: Joseph, 1952
A PROPER MARRIAGE.[1] London: Joseph, 1954
RETREAT TO INNOCENCE. London: Joseph, 1956
A RIPPLE FROM THE STORM.[1] London: Joseph, 1958

THE GOLDEN NOTEBOOK. London: Joseph, 1962
LANDLOCKED.[1] London: MacGibbon & Kee, 1965
[1]A series: CHILDREN OF VIOLENCE

C[LIVE] S[TAPLES] LEWIS (1898-1963)
THE PILGRIM'S REGRESS. London: Dent, 1933
OUT OF THE SILENT PLANET.[1] London: Lane, 1938
PERELANDRA.[1] London: Lane, 1943
THAT HIDEOUS STRENGTH.[1] London: Lane, 1945
THE GREAT DIVORCE. London: Bles, 1945
TILL WE HAVE FACES. London: Bles, 1956
[1]A trilogy

[HARRY] SINCLAIR LEWIS (1885-1951)
Nobel Prize for Literature, 1930
OUR MR. WRENN. New York: Harper, 1914
THE TRAIL OF THE HAWK. New York: Harper, 1915
THE JOB. New York: Harper, 1917
THE INNOCENTS. New York: Harper, 1917
FREE AIR. New York: Harcourt, Brace & Howe, 1919
MAIN STREET. New York: Harcourt, Brace & Howe, 1920
BABBITT. New York: Harcourt, Brace, 1922
ARROWSMITH. New York: Harcourt, Brace, 1925. London: Cape,
     1925, under the title MARTIN ARROWSMITH. *Pulitzer Prize,
     1926*
MANTRAP. New York: Harcourt, Brace, 1926
ELMER GANTRY. New York: Harcourt, Brace, 1927
THE MAN WHO KNEW COOLIDGE. New York: Harcourt, Brace,
     1928
DODSWORTH. New York: Harcourt, Brace, 1929
ANN VICKERS. Garden City: Doubleday, Doran, 1933
WORK OF ART. Garden City: Doubleday, Doran, 1934
IT CAN'T HAPPEN HERE. Garden City: Doubleday, Doran, 1935
THE PRODIGAL PARENTS. Garden City: Doubleday, Doran, 1938
BETHEL MERRIDAY. Garden City: Doubleday, Doran, 1940
GIDEON PLANISH. New York: Random House, 1943
CASS TIMBERLANE. New York: Random House, 1945
KINGSBLOOD ROYAL. New York: Random House, 1947
THE GOD-SEEKER. New York: Random House, 1949
WORLD SO WIDE. New York: Random House, 1951
STORM IN THE WEST (in collaboration with Dore Schary). New
     York: Stein & Day, 1963

[PERCY] WYNDHAM LEWIS (1884-1957)
TARR. London: Egoist, 1918

THE CHILDERMASS.[1] London: Chatto & Windus, 1928. Reissued
　　as CHILDERMASS, London: Methuen, 1956
THE APES OF GOD. London: Arthur, 1930
SNOOTY BARONET. London: Cassell, 1932
THE REVENGE FOR LOVE. London: Cassell, 1937
THE VULGAR STREAK. London: Hale, 1941
SELF CONDEMNED. London: Methuen, 1954
MONSTRE GAI.[1] London: Methuen, 1955
MALIGN FIESTA.[1] London: Methuen, 1955
THE RED PRIEST. London: Methuen, 1956
[1]A projected tetralogy (with "The Trial of Man") : THE HUMAN AGE

ERIC [ROBERT RUSSELL] LINKLATER (1899-　　)
WHITE-MAA'S SAGA. London: Cape, 1929
POET'S PUB. London: Cape, 1929
JUAN IN AMERICA. London: Cape, 1931
THE MEN OF NESS. London: Cape, 1932
MAGNUS MERRIMAN. London: Cape, 1934
RIPENESS IS ALL. London: Cape, 1935
JUAN IN CHINA. London: Cape, 1937
THE SAILOR'S HOLIDAY. London: Cape, 1937
THE IMPREGNABLE WOMEN. London: Cape, 1938
JUDAS. London: Cape, 1939
PRIVATE ANGELO. London: Cape, 1946
A SPELL FOR OLD BONES. London: Cape, 1949
MR. BYCULLA. London: Hart-Davis, 1950
LAXDALE HALL. London: Cape, 1951
THE HOUSE OF GAIR. London: Cape, 1953
THE FAITHFUL ALLY. London: Cape, 1954. New York: Har-
　　court, Brace, 1955, under the title THE SULTAN AND THE
　　LADY
THE DARK OF SUMMER. London: Cape, 1956
POSITION AT NOON. London: Cape, 1958. New York: Harcourt,
　　Brace, 1959, under the title MY FATHERS AND I
THE MERRY MUSE. London: Cape, 1959
ROLL OF HONOUR. London: Hart-Davis, 1961
HUSBAND OF DELILAH. London: Macmillan, 1962
A MAN OVER FORTY. London: Macmillan, 1963
A TERRIBLE FREEDOM. London: Macmillan, 1966

RICHARD [DAVID VIVIAN] LLEWELLYN [LLOYD] (1907-　　)
HOW GREEN WAS MY VALLEY.[1] London: Joseph, 1939

NONE BUT THE LONELY HEART. London: Joseph, 1943
A FEW FLOWERS FOR SHINER. London: Joseph, 1950
A FLAME FOR DOUBTING THOMAS. New York: Macmillan,
    1953. London: Joseph, 1954
SWEET WITCH. London: Joseph, 1955. Garden City: Doubleday,
    1955, under the title THE WITCH OF MERTHYN
THE FLAME OF HERCULES. Garden City: Doubleday, 1955.
    London: Joseph, 1957
MR. HAMISH GLEAVE. London: Joseph, 1956
WARDEN OF THE SMOKE AND BELLS. Garden City: Doubleday,
    1956. London: Joseph, 1958
CHEZ PAVAN. Garden City: Doubleday, 1958. London: Joseph,
    1959
UP, INTO THE SINGING MOUNTAIN.[1] Garden City: Doubleday,
    1960. London: Joseph, 1963
A MAN IN A MIRROR. Garden City: Doubleday, 1961. London:
    Joseph, 1964
SWEET MORN OF JUDAS' DAY. Garden City: Doubleday, 1964.
    London: Joseph, 1965
DOWN WHERE THE MOON IS SMALL.[1] London: Joseph, 1966
[1] A trilogy

ROSS [FRANKLIN] LOCKRIDGE [JR.] (1914-1948)

RAINTREE COUNTY. Boston: Houghton Mifflin, 1948

[JOHN GRIFFITH] JACK LONDON (1876-1916)

A DAUGHTER OF THE SNOWS. Philadelphia: Lippincott, 1902
THE CALL OF THE WILD. New York: Macmillan, 1903
THE SEA WOLF. New York: Macmillan, 1904
THE GAME. New York: Macmillan, 1905
WHITE FANG. New York: Macmillan, 1906
BEFORE ADAM. New York: Macmillan, 1906
THE IRON HEEL. New York: Macmillan, 1907
MARTIN EDEN. New York: Macmillan, 1909
BURNING DAYLIGHT. New York: Macmillan, 1910
ADVENTURE. New York: Macmillan, 1911
SMOKE BELLEW. New York: Century, 1912
THE ABYSMAL BRUTE. New York: Century, 1913
THE VALLEY OF THE MOON. New York: Macmillan, 1913
THE MUTINY OF THE ELSINORE. New York: Macmillan, 1914
THE SCARLET PLAGUE. New York: Macmillan, 1915
THE STAR ROVER. New York: Macmillan, 1915
THE LITTLE LADY OF THE BIG HOUSE. New York: Macmillan,
    1916

HEARTS OF THREE. New York: Macmillan, 1920
THE ASSASSINATION BUREAU, LTD. (*unfinished; completed*
by Robert L. Fish). New York: McGraw-Hill, 1963

ROGER [ERSKINE] LONGRIGG (1929-   )
A HIGH-PITCHED BUZZ. London: Faber & Faber, 1956
SWITCHBOARD. London: Faber & Faber, 1957
WRONG NUMBER. London: Faber & Faber, 1959
DAUGHTERS OF MULBERRY. London: Faber & Faber, 1961
THE PAPER BOATS. London: Faber & Faber, 1963

[CLARENCE] MALCOLM LOWRY (1909-1957)
ULTRAMARINE. London: Cape, 1933
UNDER THE VOLCANO. London: Cape, 1947

ANDREW [NELSON] LYTLE (1902-   )
THE LONG NIGHT. Indianapolis: Bobbs-Merrill, 1936
AT THE MOON'S INN. Indianapolis: Bobbs-Merrill, 1941
A NAME FOR EVIL. Indianapolis: Bobbs-Merrill, 1947
THE VELVET HORN. New York: McDowell, Obolensky, 1957

Dame ROSE MACAULAY (1881-1958)
ABBOTS VERNEY. London: Murray, 1906
THE FURNACE. London: Murray, 1907
THE SECRET RIVER. London: Murray, 1909
THE VALLEY CAPTIVES. London: Murray, 1911
VIEWS AND VAGABONDS. London: Murray, 1912
THE LEE SHORE. London: Hodder & Stoughton, 1912
THE MAKING OF A BIGOT. London: Hodder & Stoughton, 1914
NON-COMBATANTS AND OTHERS. London: Hodder & Stough-
ton, 1916
WHAT NOT. London: Constable, 1919
POTTERISM. London: Collins, 1920
DANGEROUS AGES. London: Collins, 1921. *Femina-Vie Heureuse*
Prize, 1922
MYSTERY AT GENEVA. London: Collins, 1922
TOLD BY AN IDIOT. London: Collins, 1923
ORPHAN ISLAND. London: Collins, 1924
CREWE TRAIN. London: Collins, 1926
KEEPING UP APPEARANCES. London: Collins, 1928. New York:
Boni & Liveright, 1928, under the title DAISY AND DAPHNE
STAYING WITH RELATIONS. London: Collins, 1930
THEY WERE DEFEATED. London: Collins, 1932. New York:

Harper, 1932, under the title THE SHADOW FLIES
GOING ABROAD. London: Collins, 1934
I WOULD BE PRIVATE. London: Collins, 1937
AND NO MAN'S WIT. London: Collins, 1940
THE WORLD MY WILDERNESS. London: Collins, 1950
THE TOWERS OF TREBIZOND. London: Collins, 1956. *James
Tait Black Memorial Prize, 1957*

MARY [THERESE] McCARTHY (1912-   )
THE COMPANY SHE KEEPS. New York: Simon & Schuster, 1942
THE OASIS. New York: Random House, 1949. London: Heinemann,
    1950, under the title A SOURCE OF EMBARRASSMENT
THE GROVES OF ACADEME. New York: Harcourt, Brace, 1952
A CHARMED LIFE. New York: Harcourt, Brace, 1955
THE GROUP. New York: Harcourt, Brace & World, 1963

[LULA] CARSON [SMITH] McCULLERS (1917-   )
THE HEART IS A LONELY HUNTER.[1] Boston: Houghton Mifflin,
    1940
REFLECTIONS IN A GOLDEN EYE.[1] Boston: Houghton Mifflin,
    1941
THE MEMBER OF THE WEDDING.[1] Boston: Houghton Mifflin,
    1946
CLOCK WITHOUT HANDS. Boston: Houghton Mifflin, 1961
[1]Collected (with stories) in THE BALLAD OF THE SAD CAFÉ, Boston:
    Houghton Mifflin, 1951

JOHN McGAHERN (1935-   )
THE BARRACKS. London: Faber & Faber, 1963
THE DARK. London: Faber & Faber, 1965

COLIN MacINNES (-   )
JUNE IN HER SPRING. London: MacGibbon & Kee, 1952
CITY OF SPADES. London: MacGibbon & Kee, 1957
ABSOLUTE BEGINNERS. London: MacGibbon & Kee, 1959
MR. LOVE AND JUSTICE. London: MacGibbon & Kee, 1960
ALL DAY SATURDAY. London: MacGibbon & Kee, 1966

Sir [EDWARD MONTAGUE] COMPTON MACKENZIE (1883-   )
THE PASSIONATE ELOPEMENT. London: Secker, 1911
CARNIVAL. London: Secker, 1912

SINISTER STREET, Vol. I.[1] London: Secker, 1913. New York: Appleton, 1913, under the title YOUTH'S ENCOUNTER

SINISTER STREET, Vol. II.[1] London: Secker, 1914

GUY AND PAULINE. London: Secker, 1915. New York: Harper, 1915, under the title PLASHERS MEAD

THE EARLY LIFE AND ADVENTURES OF SYLVIA SCARLETT.[2] London: Secker, 1918

SYLVIA AND MICHAEL.[2] London: Secker, 1919

POOR RELATIONS. London: Secker, 1919

THE VANITY GIRL. London: Cassell, 1920

RICH RELATIVES. London: Secker, 1921

THE ALTAR STEPS.[3] London: Cassell, 1922

THE SEVEN AGES OF WOMAN. London: Secker, 1923

THE PARSON'S PROGRESS.[3] London: Cassell, 1923

THE HEAVENLY LADDER.[3] London: Cassell, 1924

THE OLD MEN OF THE SEA. London: Cassell, 1924. Reissued as PARADISE FOR SALE, London: Macdonald, 1963

CORAL. London: Cassell, 1925

FAIRY GOLD. London: Cassell, 1926

ROGUES AND VAGADONDS. London: Cassell, 1927

VESTAL FIRE. London: Cassell, 1927

EXTREMES MEET. London: Cassell, 1928

EXTRAORDINARY WOMEN. London: Secker, 1928

THE THREE COURIERS. London: Cassell, 1929

APRIL FOOLS. London: Cassell, 1930

BUTTERCUPS AND DAISIES. London: Cassell, 1931. Garden City: Doubleday, Doran, 1931, under the title FOR SALE

OUR STREET. London: Cassell, 1931

WATER ON THE BRAIN. London: Cassell, 1933

THE DARKENING GREEN. London: Cassell, 1934

FIGURE OF EIGHT. London: Cassell, 1936

THE EAST WIND OF LOVE.[4] London: Rich & Cowan, 1937. New York: Dodd, Mead, 1937, under the title THE EAST WIND

THE SOUTH WIND OF LOVE.[4] London: Rich & Cowan, 1937

THE WEST WIND OF LOVE.[4] London: Chatto & Windus, 1940

WEST TO NORTH.[4] London: Chatto & Windus, 1940

THE RED TAPEWORM. London: Chatto & Windus, 1941

THE MONARCH OF THE GLEN. London: Chatto & Windus, 1941

KEEP THE HOME GUARD TURNING. London: Chatto & Windus, 1943

THE NORTH WIND OF LOVE, Vol. I.[4] London: Chatto & Windus, 1944

THE NORTH WIND OF LOVE, Vol. II.[4] London: Chatto &

Windus, 1945. New York: Dodd, Mead, 1946, under the title
AGAIN TO THE NORTH
WHISKY GALORE. London: Chatto & Windus, 1947. Boston:
Houghton Mifflin, 1950, under the title TIGHT LITTLE
ISLAND
HUNTING THE FAIRIES. London: Chatto & Windus, 1949
THE RIVAL MONSTER. London: Chatto & Windus, 1952
BEN NEVIS GOES EAST. London: Chatto & Windus, 1954
THIN ICE. London: Chatto & Windus, 1956
ROCKETS GALORE. London: Chatto & Windus, 1957
THE LUNATIC REPUBLIC. London: Chatto & Windus, 1959
MEZZOTINT. London: Chatto & Windus, 1961
THE STOLEN SOPRANO. London: Chatto & Windus, 1965
PAPER LIVES. London: Chatto & Windus, 1966
[1]One volume ed., 1923
[2]THE LIFE AND ADVENTURES OF SYLVIA SCARLETT, London: Secker,
1927
[3]A trilogy
[4]THE FOUR WINDS OF LOVE

[JOHN] HUGH MacLENNAN (1907-   )
BAROMETER RISING. New York: Duell, Sloan & Pearce, 1941
TWO SOLITUDES. New York: Duell, Sloan & Pearce, 1945.
Governor-General's Award, 1946
THE PRECIPICE. New York: Duell, Sloan & Pearce, 1948.
Governor-General's Award, 1949
EACH MAN'S SON. Boston: Little, Brown, 1951
THE WATCH THAT ENDS THE NIGHT. New York: Scribner,
1959. *Governor-General's Award, 1960*

NORMAN [KINGSLEY] MAILER (1923-   )
THE NAKED AND THE DEAD. New York: Rinehart, 1948
BARBARY SHORE. New York: Rinehart, 1951
THE DEER PARK. New York: Putnam, 1955
AN AMERICAN DREAM. New York: Dial, 1965

BERNARD MALAMUD (1914-   )
THE NATURAL. New York: Harcourt, Brace, 1952
THE ASSISTANT. New York: Farrar, Straus & Cudahy, 1957.
Rosenthal Award, 1958
A NEW LIFE. New York: Farrar, Straus & Cudahy, 1961
THE FIXER. New York: Farrar, Straus & Giroux, 1966. *National
Book Award, 1967. Pulitzer Prize, 1967*

MANOHAR [DATTATRAY] MALGONKAR (1913-   )

DISTANT DRUM. London: Asia Publishing House, 1961
COMBAT OF SHADOWS. London: Hamilton, 1962
THE PRINCES. London: Hamilton, 1963
A BEND IN THE GANGES. London: Hamilton, 1964

OLIVIA MANNING (-   )

THE WIND CHANGES. London: Cape, 1938
ARTIST AMONG THE MISSING. London: Heinemann, 1949
SCHOOL FOR LOVE. London: Heinemann, 1951
A DIFFERENT FACE. London: Heinemann, 1953
THE DOVES OF VENUS. London: Heinemann, 1955
THE GREAT FORTUNE.[1] London: Heinemann, 1960
THE SPOILT CITY.[1] London: Heinemann, 1962
FRIENDS AND HEROES.[1] London: Heinemann, 1965
[1]Balkan Trilogy

WILLIAM [EDWARD] MARCH [CAMPBELL] (1893-1954)

COMPANY K. New York: Smith & Haas, 1933
COME IN AT THE DOOR. New York: Smith & Haas, 1934
THE TALLONS. New York: Random House, 1936. London: Rich & Cowan, 1936, under the title A SONG FOR HARPS
THE LOOKING-GLASS. Boston: Little, Brown, 1943
OCTOBER ISLAND. Boston: Little, Brown, 1952
THE BAD SEED. New York: Rinehart, 1954

KAMALA MARKANDAYA, i.e. KAMALA PURNAIYA TAYLOR (1924-   )

NECTAR IN A SIEVE. London: Putnam, 1954
SOME INNER FURY. London: Putnam, 1955
A SILENCE OF DESIRE. London: Putnam, 1960
POSSESSION. London: Putnam, 1963
A HANDFUL OF RICE. London: Hamilton, 1966

JOHN P[HILLIPS] MARQUAND (1893-1960)

THE UNSPEAKABLE GENTLEMAN. New York: Scribner, 1922
THE BLACK CARGO. New York: Scribner, 1925
WARNING HILL. Boston: Little, Brown, 1930
HAVEN'S END. Boston: Little, Brown, 1933
MING YELLOW. Boston: Little, Brown, 1935

NO HERO. Boston: Little, Brown, 1935. London: Hale, 1940, under the title MR. MOTO TAKES A HAND
THANK YOU, MR. MOTO.[1] Boston: Little, Brown, 1936
THE LATE GEORGE APLEY.[2] Boston: Little, Brown, 1937. *Pulitzer Prize, 1938*
THINK FAST, MR. MOTO.[1] Boston: Little, Brown, 1937
MR. MOTO IS SO SORRY.[1] Boston: Little, Brown, 1938
WICKFORD POINT.[2] Boston: Little, Brown, 1939
DON'T ASK QUESTIONS. London: Hale, 1941
H. M. PULHAM, ESQUIRE.[2] Boston: Little, Brown, 1941
LAST LAUGH, MR. MOTO. Boston: Little, Brown, 1942
SO LITTLE TIME. Boston: Little, Brown, 1943
REPENT IN HASTE. Boston: Little, Brown, 1945
B. F.'S DAUGHTER. Boston: Little, Brown, 1946. London: Hale, 1947, under the title POLLY FULTON
POINT OF NO RETURN. Boston: Little, Brown, 1949
IT'S LOADED, MR. BAUER. London: Hale, 1949
MELVILLE GOODWIN, USA. Boston: Little, Brown, 1951
SINCERELY, WILLIS WAYDE. Boston: Little, Brown, 1955
STOPOVER: TOKYO. Boston: Little, Brown, 1957
WOMEN AND THOMAS HARROW. Boston: Little, Brown, 1958

[1]Collected as MR. MOTO'S THREE ACES, Boston: Little, Brown, 1956
[2]Collected as NORTH OF GRAND CENTRAL, Boston: Little, Brown, 1956

JOHN [EDWARD] MASEFIELD, O.M., C.Litt. (1878-1967)

CAPTAIN MARGARET. London: Richards, 1908
MULTITUDE AND SOLITUDE. London: Richards, 1909
THE STREET OF TO-DAY. London: Dent, 1911
THE TAKING OF HELEN. London: Heinemann, 1923
SARD HARKER. London: Heinemann, 1924
ODTAA. London: Heinemann, 1926
THE MIDNIGHT FOLK. London: Heinemann, 1927
THE HAWBUCKS. London: Heinemann, 1929
THE BIRD OF DAWNING. London: Heinemann, 1933
THE TAKING OF THE GRY. London: Heinemann, 1934
VICTORIOUS TROY. London: Heinemann, 1935
EGGS AND BAKER. London: Heinemann, 1936
THE SQUARE PEG. London: Heinemann, 1937
DEAD NED. London: Heinemann, 1938
LIVE AND KICKING NED. London: Heinemann, 1939
BASILISSA. London: Heinemann, 1940
CONQUER. London: Heinemann, 1941
BADON PARCHMENTS. London: Heinemann, 1947

PETER MATTHIESSEN (1927-   )
RACE ROCK. New York: Harper, 1954
PARTISANS. New York: Viking, 1955
RADITZER. New York: Viking, 1961
AT PLAY IN THE FIELDS OF THE LORD. New York: Random House, 1965

W[ILLIAM] SOMERSET MAUGHAM, C.Litt. (1874-1965)
LIZA OF LAMBETH. London: Unwin, 1897
THE MAKING OF A SAINT. London: Unwin, 1898
THE HERO. London: Hutchinson, 1901
MRS. CRADDOCK. London: Heinemann, 1902
THE MERRY-GO-ROUND. London: Heinemann, 1904
THE BISHOP'S APRON. London: Chapman & Hall, 1906
THE EXPLORER. London: Heinemann, 1907
THE MAGICIAN. London: Heinemann, 1908
OF HUMAN BONDAGE. London: Heinemann, 1915
THE MOON AND SIXPENCE. London: Heinemann, 1919
THE PAINTED VEIL. London: Heinemann, 1925
CAKES AND ALE. London: Heinemann, 1930
THE NARROW CORNER. London: Heinemann, 1932
THEATRE. London: Heinemann, 1937
CHRISTMAS HOLIDAY. London: Heinemann, 1939
UP AT THE VILLA. London: Heinemann, 1941
THE HOUR BEFORE THE DAWN. Garden City: Doubleday, Doran, 1942
THE RAZOR'S EDGE. London: Heinemann, 1944
THEN AND NOW. London: Heinemann, 1946
CATALINA. London: Heinemann, 1948

WILLIAM MAXWELL (1908-   )
BRIGHT CENTER OF HEAVEN. New York: Harper, 1934
THEY CAME LIKE SWALLOWS. New York: Harper, 1937
THE FOLDED LEAF. New York: Harper, 1945
TIME WILL DARKEN IT. New York: Harper, 1948
THE CHÂTEAU. New York: Knopf, 1961

[SALVATOR] AUBREY [CLARENCE] MENEN (1912-   )
THE PREVALENCE OF WITCHES. London: Chatto & Windus, 1947

THE STUMBLING STONE. London: Chatto & Windus, 1949
THE BACKWARD BRIDE. London: Chatto & Windus, 1950
THE DUKE OF GALLODORO. London: Chatto & Windus, 1952
RAMA RETOLD. London: Chatto & Windus, 1954. New York:
    Scribner, 1954, under the title THE RAMAYANA
ABODE OF LOVE. New York: Scribner, 1956. London: Chatto &
    Windus, 1957
THE FIG TREE. London: Chatto & Windus, 1959
SHELA. New York: Random House, 1962. London: Hamilton, 1963
A CONSPIRACY OF WOMEN. New York: Random House, 1965.
    London: Hamilton, 1966

JAMES A[LBERT] MICHENER (1907-   )

TALES OF THE SOUTH PACIFIC. New York: Macmillan, 1947.
    Pulitzer Prize, 1948
THE FIRES OF SPRING. New York: Random House, 1949
THE BRIDGES AT TOKO-RI. New York: Random House, 1953
SAYONARA. New York: Random House, 1954
HAWAII. New York: Random House, 1959
CARAVANS. New York: Random House, 1963
THE SOURCE. New York: Random House, 1965

STANLEY MIDDLETON (1919-   )

A SHORT ANSWER. London: New Authors, 1958
HARRIS'S REQUIEM. London: Hutchinson, 1960
A SERIOUS WOMAN. London: Hutchinson, 1961
THE JUST EXCHANGE. London: Hutchinson, 1962
TWO'S COMPANY. London: Hutchinson, 1963
HIM THEY COMPELLED. London: Hutchinson, 1964
TERMS OF REFERENCE. London: Hutchinson, 1966

HENRY [VALENTINE] MILLER (1891-   )

TROPIC OF CANCER.[1] Paris: Obelisk, 1934. New York: Grove,
    1961
BLACK SPRING.[1] Paris: Obelisk, 1936. New York: Grove, 1963
TROPIC OF CAPRICORN.[1] Paris: Obelisk, 1939. New York: Grove,
    1962
THE SMILE AT THE FOOT OF THE LADDER. New York: Duell,
    Sloan & Pearce, 1948
SEXUS.[2] Paris: Olympia, 1949. New York: Grove, 1965
PLEXUS.[2] Paris: Olympia, 1953. New York: Grove, 1965
QUIET DAYS IN CLICHY. Paris: Olympia, 1956. New York:
    Grove, 1965

NEXUS.² Paris: Obelisk, 1960. New York: Grove, 1965
¹A trilogy of "autobiographical romances"
²A trilogy: THE ROSY CRUCIFIXION

SARAH GERTRUDE [LIEBSON] MILLIN (1889-   )
THE DARK RIVER. London: Collins, 1919
MIDDLE-CLASS. London: Collins, 1921
ADAM'S REST. London: Collins, 1922
THE JORDANS. London: Collins, 1923
GOD'S STEP-CHILDREN. London: Constable, 1924
MARY GLENN. London: Constable, 1925
AN ARTIST IN THE FAMILY. London: Constable, 1928
THE COMING OF THE LORD. London: Constable, 1928
THE FIDDLER. London: Constable, 1929
THE SONS OF MRS. AAB. London: Chatto & Windus, 1931
THREE MEN DIE. London: Chatto & Windus, 1934
WHAT HATH A MAN? London: Chatto & Windus, 1938
THE HERR WITCH DOCTOR. London: Heinemann, 1941. New
    York: Harper, 1941, under the title THE DARK GODS
KING OF THE BASTARDS. London: Heinemann, 1950
THE BURNING MAN. London: Heinemann, 1952
THE WIZARD BIRD. London: Heinemann, 1962
GOODBYE, DEAR ENGLAND. London: Heinemann, 1965

J[AMES] LESLIE MITCHELL: See LEWIS GRASSIC GIBBON

JULIAN MITCHELL (1935-   )
IMAGINARY TOYS. London: New Authors, 1961
A DISTURBING INFLUENCE. London: Hutchinson, 1962
AS FAR AS YOU CAN GO. London: Constable, 1963
THE WHITE FATHER. London: Constable, 1964. *John Llewelyn
    Rhys Memorial Prize, 1965. Somerset Maugham Award, 1966*
A CIRCLE OF FRIENDS. London: Constable, 1966

MARGARET [MUNNERLYN] MITCHELL (1900-1949)
GONE WITH THE WIND. New York: Macmillan, 1936. *Pulitzer
    Prize, 1937*

NAOMI [MARGARET HALDANE] MITCHISON (1897-   )

THE CONQUERED. London: Cape, 1923
CLOUD CUCKOO LAND. London: Cape, 1925
THE CORN KING AND THE SPRING QUEEN. London: Cape, 1931
THE POWERS OF LIGHT. London: Pharos, 1932
WE HAVE BEEN WARNED. London: Constable, 1935
BEYOND THIS LIMIT. London: Cape, 1935
THE BLOOD OF THE MARTYRS. London: Constable, 1939. New York: Whittlesey House, 1948, under the title BLOOD OF THE MARTYRS
THE BULL CALVES. London: Cape, 1947
LOBSTERS ON THE AGENDA. London: Gollancz, 1952
TRAVEL LIGHT. London: Faber & Faber, 1952
TO THE CHAPEL PERILOUS. London: Allen & Unwin, 1955
BEHOLD YOUR KING. London: Muller, 1957
MEMOIRS OF A SPACE WOMAN. London: Gollancz, 1962
WHEN WE BECOME MEN. London: Collins, 1965

Hon. NANCY MITFORD (1904-   )

HIGHLAND FLING. London: Butterworth, 1931
CHRISTMAS PUDDING. London: Butterworth, 1932
WIGS ON THE GREEN. London: Butterworth, 1935
PIGEON PIE. London: Hamilton, 1940
THE PURSUIT OF LOVE. London: Hamilton, 1945
LOVE IN A COLD CLIMATE. London: Hamilton, 1949
THE BLESSING. London: Hamilton, 1951
DON'T TELL ALFRED. London: Hamilton, 1960

EDGAR [AUSTIN] MITTELHOLZER (1909-1965)

CORENTYNE THUNDER. London: Eyre & Spottiswoode, 1941
A MORNING AT THE OFFICE. London: Hogarth, 1950. Garden City: Doubleday, 1950, under the title A MORNING IN TRINIDAD
SHADOWS MOVE AMONG THEM. London: Nevill, 1951
CHILDREN OF KAYWANA. London: Nevill, 1952
THE WEATHER IN MIDDENSHOT. London: Secker & Warburg, 1952
THE LIFE AND DEATH OF SYLVIA. London: Secker & Warburg, 1953
THE HARROWING OF HUBERTUS. London: Secker & Warburg, 1954. New York: Day, 1955, under the title HUBERTUS

MY BONES AND MY FLUTE. London: Secker & Warburg, 1955
OF TREES AND THE SEA. London: Secker & Warburg, 1956
A TALE OF THREE PLACES. London: Secker & Warburg, 1957
KAYWANA BLOOD. London: Secker & Warburg, 1958. Garden
City: Doubleday, 1958, under the title THE OLD BLOOD
THE MAD MacMULLOCHS (by "H. Austin Woodsley"). London:
Owen, 1959
A TINKLING IN THE TWILIGHT. London: Secker & Warburg,
1959
LATTICED ECHOES. London: Secker & Warburg, 1960
ELTONSBRODY. London: Secker & Warburg, 1960
THUNDER RETURNING. London: Secker & Warburg, 1961
THE PILING OF THE CLOUDS. London: Putnam, 1961
THE WOUNDED AND THE WORRIED. London: Putnam, 1962
UNCLE PAUL. London: Macdonald, 1963
THE ALONENESS OF MRS. CHATHAM. London: Library 33,
1965
THE JILKINGTON DRAMA. London: Abelard-Schuman, 1965

NICHOLAS [JOHN TURNEY] MONSARRAT (1910-   )

THINK OF TO-MORROW. London: Hurst & Blackett, 1934
AT FIRST SIGHT. London: Hurst & Blackett, 1935
THE WHIPPING BOY. London: Jarrolds, 1937
THIS IS THE SCHOOLROOM. London: Cassell, 1939
THE CRUEL SEA. London: Cassell, 1951. *Heinemann Award, 1952*
THE STORY OF ESTHER COSTELLO. London: Cassell, 1953
CASTLE GARAC. London: Cassell, 1955
THE TRIBE THAT LOST ITS HEAD. London: Cassell, 1956
THE NYLON PIRATES. London: Cassell, 1960
THE WHITE RAJAH. London: Cassell, 1961
THE TIME BEFORE THIS.[1] London: Cassell, 1962
SMITH AND JONES.[1] London: Cassell, 1963
A FAIR DAY'S WORK.[1] London: Cassell, 1964
THE PILLOW FIGHT. London: Cassell, 1965
SOMETHING TO HIDE.[1] London: Cassell, 1965
[1]A series: SIGNS OF THE TIMES

C[HARLES] E[DWARD] MONTAGUE (1867-1928)

A HIND LET LOOSE. London: Methuen, 1910
THE MORNING'S WAR. London: Methuen, 1913

ROUGH JUSTICE. London: Chatto & Windus, 1926
RIGHT OFF THE MAP. London: Chatto & Windus, 1927

MARION [HOYT] MONTGOMERY [JR.] (1925-   )

THE WANDERING OF DESIRE. New York: Harper, 1962
DARRELL. Garden City: Doubleday, 1964

BRIAN MOORE (1921-   )

JUDITH HEARNE. London: Deutsch, 1955. Boston: Atlantic-Little, Brown, 1956, under the title THE LONELY PASSION OF JUDITH HEARNE. *Authors' Club First Novel Award, 1956*
THE FEAST OF LUPERCAL. Boston: Atlantic-Little, Brown, 1957. London: Deutsch, 1958
THE LUCK OF GINGER COFFEY. London: Deutsch, 1960. *Governor-General's Award, 1961*
AN ANSWER FROM LIMBO. London: Deutsch, 1962
THE EMPEROR OF ICE-CREAM. New York: Viking, 1965. London: Deutsch, 1966

CHARLES [LANGBRIDGE] MORGAN (1894-1958)

THE GUNROOM. London: Black, 1919
MY NAME IS LEGION. London: Heinemann, 1925
PORTRAIT IN A MIRROR. London: Macmillan, 1929. New York: Knopf, 1929, under the title FIRST LOVE. *Femina-Vie Heureuse Prize, 1930*
THE FOUNTAIN. London: Macmillan, 1932. *Hawthornden Prize, 1933*
SPARKENBROKE. London: Macmillan, 1936
THE VOYAGE. London: Macmillan, 1940. *James Tait Black Memorial Prize, 1941*
THE EMPTY ROOM. London: Macmillan, 1941
THE JUDGE'S STORY. London: Macmillan, 1947
THE RIVER LINE. London: Macmillan, 1949
A BREEZE OF MORNING. London: Macmillan, 1951
CHALLENGE TO VENUS. London: Macmillan, 1957

CHRISTOPHER [DARLINGTON] MORLEY (1890-1957)

PARNASSUS ON WHEELS. Garden City: Doubleday, Page, 1917
THE HAUNTED BOOKSHOP. Garden City: Doubleday, Page, 1919

KATHLEEN. Garden City: Doubleday, Page, 1920
WHERE THE BLUE BEGINS. Garden City: Doubleday, Page, 1922
PANDORA LIFTS THE LID (in collaboration with Don Marquis).
New York: Doran, 1924
THUNDER ON THE LEFT. Garden City: Doubleday, Page, 1925
PLEASED TO MEET YOU. Garden City: Doubleday, Page, 1927
RUDOLPH AND AMINA. New York: Day, 1930
SWISS FAMILY MANHATTAN. Garden City: Doubleday, Doran,
1932
HUMAN BEING. Garden City: Doubleday, Doran, 1932
THE TROJAN HORSE. Philadelphia: Lippincott, 1937
KITTY FOYLE. Philadelphia: Lippincott, 1939
THOROFARE. New York: Harcourt, Brace, 1942
THE MAN WHO MADE FRIENDS WITH HIMSELF. Garden City:
Doubleday, 1949

WRIGHT MORRIS (1910-   )
MY UNCLE DUDLEY. New York: Harcourt, Brace, 1942
THE MAN WHO WAS THERE. New York: Scribner, 1945
THE WORLD IN THE ATTIC. New York: Scribner, 1949
MAN AND BOY. New York: Knopf, 1951
THE WORKS OF LOVE. New York: Knopf, 1952
THE DEEP SLEEP. New York: Scribner, 1953
THE HUGE SEASON. New York: Viking, 1954
THE FIELD OF VISION. New York: Harcourt, Brace, 1956. *National Book Award, 1957*
LOVE AMONG THE CANNIBALS. New York: Harcourt, Brace,
1957
CEREMONY IN LONE TREE. New York: Atheneum, 1960
WHAT A WAY TO GO. New York: Atheneum, 1962
CAUSE FOR WONDER. New York: Atheneum, 1963
ONE DAY. New York: Atheneum, 1965

[WILLIAM CHARLES] CHAPMAN MORTIMER (1907-   )
A STRANGER ON THE STAIR. London: Hart-Davis, 1950
FATHER GOOSE. London: Hart-Davis, 1951. *James Tait Black Memorial Prize, 1952*
YOUNG MEN WAITING. London: Cresset, 1952
MEDITERRANEO. London: Cresset, 1955
MADRIGAL. London: Cresset, 1960

PENELOPE MORTIMER (1918-   )

A VILLA IN SUMMER. London: Joseph, 1954
THE BRIGHT PRISON. London: Joseph, 1956
DADDY'S GONE A-HUNTING. London: Joseph, 1958. New York:
    Harcourt, Brace, 1959, under the title CAVE OF ICE
THE PUMPKIN EATER. London: Hutchinson, 1962

R[ALPH] H[ALE] MOTTRAM (1883-   )

THE SPANISH FARM.[1] London: Chatto & Windus, 1924. *Hawthornden Prize, 1924*
SIXTY-FOUR, NINETY-FOUR![1] London: Chatto & Windus, 1925
THE CRIME AT VANDERLYNDEN'S.[1] London: Chatto & Windus,
    1926
OUR MR. DORMER. London: Chatto & Windus, 1927
THE ENGLISH MISS. London: Chatto & Windus, 1928
THE BOROUGHMONGER. London: Chatto & Windus, 1929
EUROPA'S BEAST. London: Chatto & Windus, 1930. New York:
    Harper, 1930, under the title A RICH MAN'S DAUGHTER
CASTLE ISLAND. London: Chatto & Windus, 1931
HOME FOR THE HOLIDAYS. London: Chatto & Windus, 1932
DAZZLE. London: Ward, Lock, 1932
THE LAME DOG. London: Chatto & Windus, 1933. Boston: Houghton Mifflin, 1933, under the title AT THE SIGN OF THE
    LAME DOG
BUMPHREY'S. London: Murray, 1934
EARLY MORNING. London: Hutchinson, 1935
FLOWER POT END. London: Murray, 1935
TIME TO BE GOING. London: Hutchinson, 1937
THERE WAS A JOLLY MILLER. London: Hutchinson, 1938
YOU CAN'T HAVE IT BACK! London: Hutchinson, 1939
MISS LAVINGTON. London: Hutchinson, 1939
THE GHOST AND THE MAIDEN. London: Hutchinson, 1940
THE WORLD TURNS SLOWLY ROUND. London: Hutchinson,
    1942
THE CORBELLS AT WAR. London: Hutchinson, 1943
VISIT OF THE PRINCESS. London: Hutchinson, 1946
THE GENTLEMAN OF LEISURE. London: Hutchinson, 1948
COME TO THE BOWER. London: Hutchinson, 1949
ONE HUNDRED AND TWENTY-EIGHT WITNESSES. London:
    Hutchinson, 1951
THE PART THAT IS MISSING. London: Hutchinson, 1952
OVER THE WALL. London: Hutchinson, 1955
SCENES THAT ARE BRIGHTEST. London: Hutchinson, 1956

NO ONE WILL EVER KNOW. London: Hutchinson, 1958
YOUNG MAN'S FANCIES. London: Hutchinson, 1959
MUSETTA. London: Hutchinson, 1960
TIME'S INCREASE. London: Hutchinson, 1961
TO HELL, WITH CRABB ROBINSON. London: Hutchinson, 1962
HAPPY BIRDS. London: Hutchinson, 1964
MAGGIE MacKENZIE. London: Hutchinson. 1965
[1]THE SPANISH FARM TRILOGY, London: Chatto & Windus, 1927

H[ECTOR] H[UGH] MUNRO: See SAKI

[JEAN] IRIS MURDOCH (1919-   )
UNDER THE NET. London: Chatto & Windus, 1954
THE FLIGHT FROM THE ENCHANTER. London: Chatto & Windus, 1956
THE SANDCASTLE. London: Chatto & Windus, 1957
THE BELL. London: Chatto & Windus, 1958
A SEVERED HEAD. London: Chatto & Windus, 1961
AN UNOFFICIAL ROSE. London: Chatto & Windus, 1962
THE UNICORN. London: Chatto & Windus, 1963
THE ITALIAN GIRL. London: Chatto & Windus, 1964
THE RED AND THE GREEN. London: Chatto & Windus, 1965
THE TIME OF THE ANGELS. London: Chatto & Windus, 1966

L[EOPOLD] H[AMILTON] MYERS (1881-1944)
THE ORISSERS. London: Putnam, 1922
THE 'CLIO'. London: Putnam, 1925
THE NEAR AND THE FAR.[1] London: Cape, 1929
PRINCE JALI.[1] London: Cape, 1931
THE ROOT AND THE FLOWER.[2] London: Cape, 1935. *James Tait Black Memorial Prize, 1936. Femina-Vie Heureuse Prize, 1936*
STRANGE GLORY. London: Putnam, 1936
THE POOL OF VISHNU.[3] London: Cape, 1940
[1]Collected in THE ROOT AND THE FLOWER
[2]A trilogy: adds RAJAH AMAR
[3]With THE ROOT AND THE FLOWER a tetralogy: THE NEAR AND THE FAR, London: Cape, 1943

VLADIMIR [VLADIMIROVICH] NABOKOV (1899-   )
THE REAL LIFE OF SEBASTIAN KNIGHT. Norfolk, Conn.: New Directions, 1941
BEND SINISTER. New York: Holt, 1947

LOLITA. Paris: Olympia, 1955. New York: Putnam, 1958
PNIN. Garden City: Doubleday, 1957
PALE FIRE. New York: Putnam, 1962
Translated from the Russian:
CAMERA OBSCURA. London: Long, 1936. Another version:
    LAUGHTER IN THE DARK, Indianapolis: Bobbs-Merrill, 1938
DESPAIR. London: Long, 1937. Another version: under the same
    title, New York: Putnam, 1966
INVITATION TO A BEHEADING. New York: Putnam, 1959
THE GIFT. New York: Putnam, 1963
THE DEFENSE. New York: Putnam, 1964
THE EYE. New York: Phaedra, 1965

V[IDIADHAR] S[URAJPRASAD] NAIPAUL (1932-)

THE MYSTIC MASSEUR. London: Deutsch, 1957. *John Llewelyn Rhys Memorial Prize, 1958*
THE SUFFRAGE OF ELVIRA. London: Deutsch, 1958
MIGUEL STREET. London: Deutsch, 1959. *Somerset Maugham Award, 1961*
A HOUSE FOR MR. BISWAS. London: Deutsch, 1961
MR. STONE AND THE KNIGHTS COMPANION. London: Deutsch, 1963. *Hawthornden Prize, 1964*

R. K. NARAYAN (1906-)

SWAMI AND FRIENDS. London: Hamilton, 1935
THE BACHELOR OF ARTS. London: Nelson, 1937
THE DARK ROOM. London: Macmillan, 1938
THE ENGLISH TEACHER. London: Eyre & Spottiswoode, 1945.
    East Lansing: Michigan State, 1953, under the title GRATEFUL
    TO LIFE AND DEATH
MR. SAMPATH. London: Eyre & Spottiswooode, 1949. East
    Lansing: Michigan State, 1957, under the title THE PRINTER
    OF MALGUDI
THE FINANCIAL EXPERT. London: Methuen, 1952
WAITING FOR THE MAHATMA. London: Methuen, 1955
THE GUIDE. London: Methuen, 1958
THE MAN-EATER OF MALGUDI. New York: Viking, 1961. London: Heinemann, 1962

ROBERT [GRUNTAL] NATHAN (1894-)

PETER KINDRED. New York: Duffield, 1919
AUTUMN. New York: McBride, 1921

THE PUPPET MASTER. New York: McBride, 1923
JONAH. New York: McBride, 1925. London: Heinemann, 1925,
     under the title SON OF AMITTAI
THE FIDDLER IN BARLY.[1] New York: McBride, 1926
THE WOODCUTTER'S HOUSE.[1] Indianapolis: Bobbs-Merrill, 1927
THE BISHOP'S WIFE.[1] Indianapolis: Bobbs-Merrill, 1928
THERE IS ANOTHER HEAVEN.[1] Indianapolis: Bobbs-Merrill,
     1929
THE ORCHID.[1] Indianapolis: Bobbs-Merrill, 1931
ONE MORE SPRING. New York: Knopf, 1933
ROAD OF AGES. New York: Knopf, 1935
THE ENCHANTED VOYAGE. New York: Knopf, 1936
WINTER IN APRIL. New York: Knopf, 1938
JOURNEY OF TAPIOLA.[2] New York: Knopf, 1938
PORTRAIT OF JENNIE. New York: Knopf, 1940
TAPIOLA'S BRAVE REGIMENT.[2] New York: Knopf, 1941
THEY WENT ON TOGETHER. New York: Knopf, 1941
THE SEA-GULL CRY. New York: Knopf, 1942
BUT GENTLY DAY. New York: Knopf, 1943
MR. WHITTLE AND THE MORNING STAR. New York: Knopf,
     1947
LONG AFTER SUMMER. New York: Knopf, 1948
THE RIVER JOURNEY. New York: Knopf, 1949
THE MARRIED LOOK. New York: Knopf, 1950. London: Staples,
     1951, under the title HIS WIFE'S YOUNG FACE
THE INNOCENT EVE. New York: Knopf, 1951
THE TRAIN IN THE MEADOW. New York: Knopf, 1953
SIR HENRY. New York: Knopf, 1955
THE RANCHO OF THE LITTLE LOVES. New York: Knopf, 1956
SO LOVE RETURNS. New York: Knopf, 1958
THE COLOR OF EVENING. New York: Knopf, 1960
THE WILDERNESS-STONE. New York: Knopf, 1961
A STAR IN THE WIND. New York: Knopf, 1962
THE DEVIL WITH LOVE. New York: Knopf, 1963
THE FAIR. New York: Knopf, 1964
THE MALLOT DIARIES. New York: Knopf, 1965
[1]Collected as THE BARLY FIELDS, New York: Knopf, 1938
[2]THE ADVENTURES OF TAPIOLA, New York: Knopf, 1950

HOWARD NEMEROV (1920-   )

THE MELODRAMATISTS. New York: Random House, 1949
FEDERIGO. Boston: Little, Brown, 1954
THE HOMECOMING GAME. New York: Simon & Schuster, 1957

P[ERCY] H[OWARD] NEWBY (1918-   )

A JOURNEY TO THE INTERIOR. London: Cape, 1945. *Somerset Maugham Award, 1948*
AGENTS AND WITNESSES. London: Cape, 1947
MARINER DANCES. London: Cape, 1948
THE SNOW PASTURE. London: Cape, 1949
THE YOUNG MAY MOON. London: Cape, 1950
A SEASON IN ENGLAND. London: Cape, 1951
A STEP TO SILENCE. London: Cape, 1952
THE RETREAT. London: Cape, 1953
THE PICNIC AT SAKKARA. London: Cape, 1955
REVOLUTION AND ROSES. London: Cape, 1957
A GUEST AND HIS GOING. London: Cape, 1959
THE BARBARY LIGHT. London: Faber & Faber, 1962
ONE OF THE FOUNDERS. London: Faber & Faber, 1965

CHARLES NORDEN: See LAWRENCE [GEORGE] DURRELL

[BENJAMIN] FRANK[LIN] NORRIS (1870-1902)

MORAN OF THE LADY LETTY. New York: Doubleday & McClure, 1898. London: Richards, 1899, under the title SHANGHAIED
McTEAGUE. New York: Doubleday & McClure, 1899
BLIX. New York: Doubleday & McClure, 1899
A MAN'S WOMAN. New York: Doubleday & McClure, 1900
THE OCTOPUS.[1] New York: Doubleday, Page, 1901
THE PIT.[1] New York: Doubleday, Page, 1903
VANDOVER AND THE BRUTE. Garden City: Doubleday, Page, 1914

[1]A projected trilogy (with "The Wolf"): THE EPIC OF THE WHEAT

EDNA O'BRIEN (1932-   )

THE COUNTRY GIRLS. London: Hutchinson, 1960
THE LONELY GIRL. London: Cape, 1962
GIRLS IN THEIR MARRIED BLISS. London: Cape, 1964
AUGUST IS A WICKED MONTH. London: Cape, 1965
CASUALTIES OF PEACE. London: Cape, 1966

FLANN O'BRIEN, i.e. BRIAN O'NOLAN (1911-1966)

AT SWIM-TWO-BIRDS. London: Longmans, 1939
THE HARD LIFE. London: MacGibbon & Kee, 1961
THE DALKEY ARCHIVE. London: MacGibbon & Kee, 1964

KATE O'BRIEN (1897-   )

WITHOUT MY CLOAK. London: Heinemann, 1931. *James Tait Black Memorial Prize, 1932. Hawthornden Prize, 1932*
THE ANTE-ROOM. London: Heinemann, 1934
MARY LAVELLE. London: Heinemann, 1936
PRAY FOR THE WANDERER. London: Heinemann, 1938
THE LAND OF SPICES. London: Heinemann, 1941
THE LAST OF SUMMER. London: Heinemann, 1943
THAT LADY. London: Heinemann, 1946. Garden City: Doubleday, 1946, under the title FOR ONE SWEET GRAPE
THE FLOWER OF MAY. London: Heinemann, 1953
AS MUSIC AND SPLENDOUR. London: Heinemann, 1958

EDWIN [GREENE] O'CONNOR (1918-   )

THE ORACLE. New York: Harper, 1951
THE LAST HURRAH. Boston: Atlantic-Little, Brown, 1956
BENJY. Boston: Atlantic-Little, Brown, 1957
THE EDGE OF SADNESS. Boston: Atlantic-Little, Brown, 1961. *Pulitzer Prize, 1962*
I WAS DANCING. Boston: Atlantic-Little, Brown, 1964
ALL IN THE FAMILY. Boston: Atlantic-Little, Brown, 1966

[MARY] FLANNERY O'CONNOR (1925-1964)

WISE BLOOD. New York: Harcourt, Brace, 1952
THE VIOLENT BEAR IT AWAY. New York: Farrar, Straus & Cudahy, 1960

SEAN O'FAOLAIN (1900-   )

A NEST OF SIMPLE FOLK. London: Cape, 1933
BIRD ALONE. London: Cape, 1936
COME BACK TO ERIN. London: Cape, 1940

LIAM O'FLAHERTY (1897-   )

THY NEIGHBOUR'S WIFE. London: Cape, 1923
THE BLACK SOUL. London: Cape, 1924
THE INFORMER. London: Cape, 1925. *James Tait Black Memorial Prize, 1926*
MR. GILHOOLEY. London: Cape, 1926
THE ASSASSIN. London: Cape, 1928
THE HOUSE OF GOLD. London: Cape, 1929
RETURN OF THE BRUTE. London: Mandrake, 1929
THE PURITAN. London: Cape, 1931

SKERRETT. London: Gollancz, 1932
THE MARTYR. London: Gollancz, 1933
HOLLYWOOD CEMETERY. London: Gollancz, 1935
FAMINE. London: Gollancz, 1937
LAND. London: Gollancz, 1946
INSURRECTION. London: Gollancz, 1950

JOHN [HENRY] O'HARA (1905-   )

Award of Merit Medal for the Novel, American Academy of Arts
    and Letters, 1964
APPOINTMENT IN SAMARRA. New York: Harcourt, Brace, 1934
BUTTERFIELD 8. New York: Harcourt, Brace, 1935
HOPE OF HEAVEN. New York: Harcourt, Brace, 1938
PAL JOEY. New York: Duell, Sloan & Pearce, 1940
A RAGE TO LIVE. New York: Random House, 1949
THE FARMERS HOTEL. New York: Random House, 1951
TEN NORTH FREDERICK. New York: Random House, 1955.
    National Book Award, 1956
A FAMILY PARTY. New York: Random House, 1956
FROM THE TERRACE. New York: Random House, 1958
OURSELVES TO KNOW. New York: Random House, 1960
SERMONS AND SODA-WATER:
    THE GIRL ON THE BAGGAGE TRUCK
    IMAGINE KISSING KATE
    WE'RE FRIENDS AGAIN.
        New York: Random House, 1960
THE BIG LAUGH. New York: Random House, 1962
ELIZABETH APPLETON. New York: Random House, 1963
THE LOCKWOOD CONCERN. New York: Random House, 1965

[GEORGE] OLIVER ONIONS (1873-1961)

THE COMPLEAT BACHELOR. London: Murray, 1900
THE ODD-JOB MAN. London: Murray, 1903
THE DRAKESTONE. London: Hurst & Blackett, 1906
PEDLAR'S PACK. London: Nash, 1908
LITTLE DEVIL DOUBT. London: Murray, 1909
THE EXCEPTION. London: Methuen, 1910
GOOD BOY SELDOM. London: Methuen, 1911
IN ACCORDANCE WITH THE EVIDENCE.[1] London: Secker,
    1912
THE DEBIT ACCOUNT.[1] London: Secker, 1913
THE STORY OF LOUIE.[1] London: Secker, 1913
THE TWO KISSES.[2] London: Methuen, 1913

A CROOKED MILE.[2] London: Methuen, 1914
MUSHROOM TOWN. London: Hodder & Stoughton, 1914
THE NEW MOON. London: Hodder & Stoughton, 1918
A CASE IN CAMERA. Bristol: Arrowsmith, 1920
THE TOWER OF OBLIVION. London: Hodder & Stoughton, 1921
PEACE IN OUR TIME. London: Chapman & Hall, 1923
THE SPITE OF HEAVEN. London: Chapman & Hall, 1925
CUT FLOWERS. London: Chapman & Hall, 1927
THE OPEN SECRET. London: Heinemann, 1930
A CERTAIN MAN. London: Heinemann, 1931
CATALAN CIRCUS. London: Nicholson & Watson, 1934
THE HAND OF KORNELIUS VOYT. London: Hamilton, 1939
COCKCROW. London: Hamilton, 1940
THE STORY OF RAGGED ROBYN. London: Joseph, 1945
POOR MAN'S TAPESTRY. London: Joseph, 1946. *James Tait Black Memorial Prize, 1947*
ARRAS OF YOUTH. London: Joseph, 1949
A PENNY FOR THE HARP. London: Joseph, 1952
A SHILLING TO SPEND. London: Joseph, 1965
[1]A trilogy: WHOM GOD HATH SUNDERED, London: Secker, 1925
[2]CRAY YOUTH, New York: Doran, 1911

BRIAN O'NOLAN: See FLANN O'BRIEN

GEORGE ORWELL, i.e. ERIC ARTHUR BLAIR (1903-1950)
BURMESE DAYS. New York: Harper, 1934. London: Gollancz, 1935
A CLERGYMAN'S DAUGHTER. London: Gollancz, 1935
KEEP THE ASPIDISTRA FLYING. London: Gollancz, 1936
COMING UP FOR AIR. London: Gollancz, 1939
ANIMAL FARM. London: Secker & Warburg, 1945
NINETEEN EIGHTY-FOUR. London: Secker & Warburg, 1949

A. R. P—M: See JOHN GALSWORTHY

EDD WINFIELD PARKS (1906-   )
BACKWATER. New York: Twayne, 1957
NASHOBA. New York: Twayne, 1963

ALAN [STEWART] PATON (1903-   )
CRY, THE BELOVED COUNTRY. London: Cape, 1948
TOO LATE THE PHALAROPE. London: Cape, 1953

WALKER PERCY (1916-   )
THE MOVIEGOER. New York: Knopf, 1961. *National Book Award, 1962*
THE LAST GENTLEMAN. New York: Farrar, Straus & Giroux, 1966

TRUMAN STRECKFUS PERSONS: See TRUMAN CAPOTE

JULIA [MOOD] PETERKIN (1880-1961)
BLACK APRIL. Indianapolis: Bobbs-Merrill, 1927
SCARLET SISTER MARY. Indianapolis: Bobbs-Merrill, 1928. *Pulitzer Prize, 1929*
BRIGHT SKIN. Indianapolis: Bobbs-Merrill, 1932

THOMAS HAL PHILLIPS (1922-   )
THE BITTERWEED PATH. New York: Rinehart, 1950
THE GOLDEN LIE. New York: Rinehart, 1951
SEARCH FOR A HERO. New York: Rinehart, 1952
KANGAROO HOLLOW. London: Allen, 1954
THE LOVED AND THE UNLOVED. New York: Harper, 1955

WILLIAM [CHARLES FRANKLYN] PLOMER (1903-   )
TURBOTT WOLFE. London: Hogarth, 1925
SADO. London: Hogarth, 1931. New York: Coward-McCann, 1932, under the title THEY NEVER CAME BACK
THE CASE IS ALTERED. London: Hogarth, 1932
THE INVADERS. London: Cape, 1934
MUSEUM PIECES. London: Cape, 1952

ERNEST POOLE (1880-1950)
THE VOICE OF THE STREET. New York: Barnes, 1906
THE HARBOR. New York: Macmillan, 1915
HIS FAMILY. New York: Macmillan, 1917. *Pulitzer Prize, 1918*
HIS SECOND WIFE. New York: Macmillan, 1918
BLIND. New York: Macmillan, 1920
BEGGARS' GOLD. New York: Macmillan, 1921
MILLIONS. New York: Macmillan, 1922
DANGER. New York: Macmillan, 1923
THE AVALANCHE. New York: Macmillan, 1924

THE HUNTER'S MOON. New York: Macmillan, 1925
WITH EASTERN EYES. New York: Macmillan, 1926
SILENT STORMS. New York: Macmillan, 1927
THE CAR OF CROESUS. New York: Macmillan, 1930
THE DESTROYER. New York: Macmillan, 1931
GREAT WINDS. New York: Macmillan, 1933
ONE OF US. New York: Macmillan, 1934
THE NANCY FLIER. New York: Crowell, 1949

KATHERINE ANNE PORTER (1890-   )
Emerson-Thoreau Medal, American Academy of Arts and Sciences,
1962. Gold Medal for Fiction, National Institute of Arts and
Letters, 1967
SHIP OF FOOLS. Boston: Atlantic-Little, Brown, 1962

ANTHONY [DYMOKE] POWELL (1905-   )
AFTERNOON MEN. London: Duckworth, 1931
VENUSBERG. London: Duckworth, 1932
FROM A VIEW TO A DEATH. London: Duckworth, 1933
AGENTS AND PATIENTS. London: Duckworth, 1936
WHAT'S BECOME OF WARING. London: Cassell, 1939
A QUESTION OF UPBRINGING.[1,2] London: Heinemann, 1951
A BUYER'S MARKET.[1,2] London: Heinemann, 1952
THE ACCEPTANCE WORLD.[1,2] London: Heinemann, 1955
AT LADY MOLLY'S.[1,3] London: Heinemann, 1957. *James Tait
Black Memorial Prize, 1958*
CASANOVA'S CHINESE RESTAURANT.[1,3] London: Heinemann,
1960
THE KINDLY ONES.[1,3] London: Heinemann, 1962
THE VALLEY OF BONES.[1] London: Heinemann, 1964
THE SOLDIER'S ART.[1] London: Heinemann, 1966
[1]A series: THE MUSIC OF TIME
[2]Collected as A DANCE TO THE MUSIC OF TIME, London: Heinemann,
1962
[3]Collected as A DANCE TO THE MUSIC OF TIME: SECOND MOVEMENT,
Boston: Little, Brown, 1964

DAWN POWELL (1897-1965)
WHITHER. Boston: Small, Maynard, 1925
SHE WALKS IN BEAUTY. New York: Brentano's, 1928
THE BRIDE'S HOUSE. New York: Brentano's, 1929
DANCE NIGHT. New York: Farrar & Rinehart, 1930
THE TENTH MOON. New York: Farrar & Rinehart, 1932

THE STORY OF A COUNTRY BOY. New York: Farrar & Rinehart, 1934
TURN, MAGIC WHEEL. New York: Farrar & Rinehart, 1936
THE HAPPY ISLAND. New York: Farrar & Rinehart, 1938
ANGELS ON TOAST. New York: Scribner, 1940
A TIME TO BE BORN. New York: Scribner, 1942
MY HOME IS FAR AWAY. New York: Scribner, 1944
THE LOCUSTS HAVE NO KING. New York: Scribner, 1948
THE WICKED PAVILION. Boston: Houghton Mifflin, 1954
A CAGE FOR LOVERS. Boston: Houghton Mifflin, 1957
THE GOLDEN SPUR. New York: Viking, 1962

J[AMES] F[ARL] POWERS (1917-   )
MORTE D'URBAN. Garden City: Doubleday, 1962. *National Book Award, 1963*

JOHN COWPER POWYS (1872-1963)
WOOD AND STONE. New York: Shaw, 1915. London: Heinemann, 1917
RODMOOR. New York: Shaw, 1916
DUCDAME. London: Heinemann, 1925
WOLF SOLENT. London: Cape, 1929
A GLASTONBURY ROMANCE. New York: Simon & Schuster, 1932. London: Lane, 1933
WEYMOUTH SANDS. New York: Simon & Schuster, 1934. London: Lane, 1935, under the title JOBBER SKALD (*expurgated*). Reissued (*unexpurgated*) under original title, London: Macdonald, 1963
MAIDEN CASTLE. New York: Simon & Schuster, 1936. London: Cassell, 1937
MORWYN. London: Cassell, 1937
OWEN GLENDOWER. New York: Simon & Schuster, 1940. London: Lane, 1941
PORIUS. London: Macdonald, 1951
THE INMATES. London: Macdonald, 1952
ATLANTIS. London: Macdonald, 1954
THE BRAZEN HEAD. London: Macdonald, 1956
HOMER AND THE AETHER. London: Macdonald, 1959
ALL OR NOTHING. London: Macdonald, 1960

T[HEODORE] F[RANCIS] POWYS (1875-1953)
BLACK BRYONY. London: Chatto & Windus, 1923
MARK ONLY. London: Chatto & Windus, 1924

MR. TASKER'S GODS. London: Chatto & Windus, 1925
MOCKERY GAP. London: Chatto & Windus, 1925
INNOCENT BIRDS. London: Chatto & Windus, 1926
MR. WESTON'S GOOD WINE. London: Chatto & Windus, 1927
KINDNESS IN A CORNER. London: Chatto & Windus, 1930
UNCLAY. London: Chatto & Windus, 1931

H[ILDA] F[RANCES] M[ARGARET] PRESCOTT (1896-   )

THE UNHURRYING CHASE. London: Constable, 1925
THE LOST FIGHT. London: Constable, 1928
SON OF DUST. London: Constable, 1932
DEAD AND NOT BURIED. London: Constable, 1938
THE MAN ON A DONKEY. London: Eyre & Spottiswoode, 1952

[EDWARD] REYNOLDS PRICE (1933-   )

A SHORT AND HAPPY LIFE. New York: Atheneum, 1962. *William Faulkner Foundation Award, 1963*
A GENEROUS MAN. New York: Atheneum, 1966

J[OHN] B[OYNTON] PRIESTLEY (1894-   )

ADAM IN MOONSHINE. London: Heinemann, 1927
BENIGHTED. London: Heinemann, 1927. New York: Harper, 1928, under the title THE OLD DARK HOUSE
FARTHING HALL (in collaboration with Hugh Walpole). London: Macmillan, 1929
THE GOOD COMPANIONS. London: Macmillan, 1929. *James Tait Black Memorial Prize, 1930*
ANGEL PAVEMENT. London: Heinemann, 1930
FARAWAY. London: Heinemann, 1932
I'LL TELL YOU EVERYTHING (in collaboration with Gerald Bullet). London: Heinemann, 1933
WONDER HERO. London: Heinemann, 1933
ALBERT GOES THROUGH. London: Heinemann, 1933
THEY WALK IN THE CITY. London: Heinemann, 1936
THE DOOMSDAY MEN. London: Heinemann, 1938
LET THE PEOPLE SING. London: Heinemann, 1939
BLACK-OUT IN GRETLEY. London: Heinemann, 1942
DAYLIGHT ON SATURDAY. London: Heinemann, 1943
THREE MEN IN NEW SUITS. London: Heinemann, 1945
BRIGHT DAY. London: Heinemann, 1946
JENNY VILLIERS. London: Heinemann, 1947

FESTIVAL AT FARBRIDGE. London: Heinemann, 1951. New
    York: Harper, 1951, under the title FESTIVAL
THE MAGICIANS. London: Heinemann, 1954
LOW NOTES ON A HIGH LEVEL. London: Heinemann, 1954
SATURN OVER THE WATER. London: Heinemann, 1961
THE THIRTY-FIRST OF JUNE. London: Heinemann, 1961
THE SHADES OF SLEEP. London: Heinemann, 1962
SIR MICHAEL AND SIR GEORGE. London: Heinemann, 1964
LOST EMPIRES. London: Heinemann, 1965
SALT IS LEAVING. London: Pan Books, 1966

V[ICTOR] S[AWDON] PRITCHETT (1900-   )
CLARE DRUMMER. London: Benn, 1929
SHIRLEY SANZ. London: Gollancz, 1932. Boston: Little, Brown,
    1932, under the title ELOPEMENT INTO EXILE
NOTHING LIKE LEATHER. London: Chatto & Windus, 1935
DEAD MAN LEADING. London: Chatto & Windus, 1937
MR. BELUNCLE. London: Chatto & Windus, 1951
THE KEY TO MY HEART. London: Chatto & Windus, 1963

FREDERIC PROKOSCH (1908-   )
THE ASIATICS. New York: Harper, 1935
THE SEVEN WHO FLED. New York: Harper, 1937. *Harper Prize,
    1937*
NIGHT OF THE POOR. New York: Harper, 1939
THE SKIES OF EUROPE. New York: Harper, 1941
THE CONSPIRATORS. New York: Harper, 1943
AGE OF THUNDER. New York: Harper, 1945
THE IDOLS OF THE CAVE. Garden City: Doubleday, 1946
STORM AND ECHO. Garden City: Doubleday, 1948
NINE DAYS TO MUKULLA. New York: Viking, 1953
A TALE FOR MIDNIGHT. Boston: Little, Brown, 1955
A BALLAD OF LOVE. New York: Farrar, Straus & Cudahy, 1960
THE SEVEN SISTERS. New York: Farrar, Straus & Cudahy, 1962
THE DARK DANCER. New York: Farrar, Straus, 1964
THE WRECK OF THE CASSANDRA. New York: Farrar, Straus &
    Giroux, 1966

PROSPERO & CALIBAN: See FREDERICK [WILLIAM SERAFINO AUSTIN LEWIS MARY] ROLFE

JAMES [OTIS] PURDY (1923-   )
MALCOLM. New York: Farrar, Straus & Cudahy, 1959

THE NEPHEW. New York: Farrar, Straus & Cudahy, 1960
CABOT WRIGHT BEGINS. New York: Farrar, Straus & Giroux, 1964

THOMAS PYNCHON (1936-   )
V. Philadelphia: Lippincott, 1963. *William Faulkner Foundation Award, 1964*
THE CRYING OF LOT 49. Philadelphia: Lippincott, 1966. *Rosenthal Award, 1967*

RAJA RAO (1909-   )
KANTHAPURA. London: Allen & Unwin, 1938
THE SERPENT AND THE ROPE. London: Murray, 1960
THE CAT AND SHAKESPEARE. New York: Macmillan, 1965

BALACHANDRA RAJAN (1920-   )
THE DARK DANCER. New York: Simon & Schuster, 1958. London: Heinemann, 1959
TOO LONG IN THE WEST. London: Heinemann, 1961

FREDERIC [MICHAEL] RAPHAEL (1931-   )
OBBLIGATO. London: Macmillan, 1956
THE EARLSDON WAY. London: Cassell, 1958
THE LIMITS OF LOVE. London: Cassell, 1960
A WILD SURMISE. London: Cassell, 1961
THE GRADUATE WIFE. London: Cassell, 1962
THE TROUBLE WITH ENGLAND. London: Cassell, 1962
LINDMANN. London: Cassell, 1963
DARLING. London: Collins, 1965

MARJORIE KINNAN RAWLINGS (1896-1953)
SOUTH MOON UNDER. New York: Scribner, 1933
GOLDEN APPLES. New York: Scribner, 1935
THE YEARLING. New York: Scribner, 1938. *Pulitzer Prize, 1939*
THE SOJOURNER. New York: Scribner, 1953

ELIOT REED: See ERIC AMBLER

FORREST REID (1876-1947)
THE KINGDOM OF TWILIGHT. London: Unwin, 1904
THE GARDEN GOD. London: Nutt, 1905

THE BRACKNELS. London: Arnold, 1911. Reissued as DENIS
    BRACKNEL, London: Faber & Faber, 1947
FOLLOWING DARKNESS. London: Arnold, 1912. Reissued as
    PETER WARING, London: Faber & Faber, 1937
THE GENTLE LOVER. London: Arnold, 1913
AT THE DOOR OF THE GATE. London: Arnold, 1915
THE SPRING SONG. London: Arnold, 1916
PIRATES OF THE SPRING. Dublin: Talbot; London: Unwin,
    1919
PENDER AMONG THE RESIDENTS. London: Collins, 1922
DEMOPHON. London: Collins, 1927
UNCLE STEPHEN.[1] London: Faber & Faber, 1931
BRIAN WESTBY. London: Faber & Faber, 1934
THE RETREAT.[1] London: Faber & Faber, 1936
YOUNG TOM.[1] London: Faber & Faber, 1944. *James Tait Black
    Memorial Prize, 1945*
[1]A trilogy: TOM BARBER, New York: Pantheon, 1955

V[ICTOR] S[TAFFORD] REID (1913-   )
NEW DAY. New York: Knopf, 1949. London: Heinemann, 1950
THE LEOPARD. London: Heinemann, 1958

MARY RENAULT, i.e. MARY CHALLANS (1905-   )
PURPOSES OF LOVE. London: Longmans, 1939. New York: Mor-
    row, 1939, under the title PROMISE OF LOVE
KIND ARE HER ANSWERS. London: Longmans, 1940
THE FRIENDLY YOUNG LADIES. London: Longmans, 1944. New
    York: Morrow, 1945, under the title THE MIDDLE MIST
RETURN TO NIGHT. London: Longmans, 1947
NORTH FACE. London: Longmans, 1948
THE CHARIOTEER. London: Longmans, 1953
THE LAST OF THE WINE. London: Longmans, 1956
THE KING MUST DIE. London: Longmans, 1958
THE BULL FROM THE SEA. London: Longmans, 1962
THE MASK OF APOLLO. London: Longmans, 1966

BARBARA RICH: See ROBERT [VON RANKE] GRAVES

DOROTHY M[ILLER] RICHARDSON (1882-1957)
POINTED ROOFS. London: Duckworth, 1915

BACKWATER. London: Duckworth, 1916
HONEYCOMB. London: Duckworth, 1917
THE TUNNEL. London: Duckworth, 1919
INTERIM. London: Duckworth, 1919
DEADLOCK. London: Duckworth, 1921
REVOLVING LIGHTS. London: Duckworth, 1923
THE TRAP. London: Duckworth, 1925
OBERLAND. London: Duckworth, 1927
DAWN'S LEFT HAND. London: Duckworth, 1931
CLEAR HORIZON. London: Dent; London: Cresset, 1935
DIMPLE HILL. London: Dent; London: Cresset, 1938
All these novels from a sequence: PILGRIMAGE, 4 vols., London: Dent;
London: Cresset, 1938

HENRY HANDEL RICHARDSON, i.e. HENRIETTA RICHARDSON ROBERTSON (1870-1946)

MAURICE GUEST. London: Heinemann, 1908
THE GETTING OF WISDOM. London: Heinemann, 1910
THE FORTUNES OF RICHARD MAHONY.[1] London: Heinemann,
1917. Reissued as AUSTRALIA FELIX, London: Heinemann,
1930
THE WAY HOME.[1] London: Heinemann, 1925
ULTIMA THULE.[1] London: Heinemann, 1929
THE YOUNG COSIMA. London: Heinemann, 1939

[1]A trilogy: THE FORTUNES OF RICHARD MAHONY, London: Heinemann, 1930

CONRAD [MICHAEL] RICHTER (1890-   )

THE SEA OF GRASS. New York: Knopf, 1937
THE TREES.[1] New York: Knopf, 1940
TACEY CROMWELL. New York: Knopf, 1942
THE FREE MAN. New York: Knopf, 1943
THE FIELDS.[1] New York: Knopf, 1946
ALWAYS YOUNG AND FAIR. New York: Knopf, 1947
THE TOWN.[1] New York: Knopf, 1950. *Pulitzer Prize, 1951*
THE LIGHT IN THE FOREST. New York: Knopf, 1953
THE LADY. New York: Knopf, 1957
THE WATERS OF KRONOS. New York: Knopf, 1960. *National
Book Award, 1961*
A SIMPLE HONORABLE MAN. New York: Knopf, 1962
THE GRANDFATHERS. New York: Knopf, 1964
A COUNTRY OF STRANGERS. New York: Knopf, 1966

[1]A trilogy: THE AWAKENING LAND, New York: Knopf, 1966

ELIZABETH MADOX ROBERTS (1886-1941)
THE TIME OF MAN. New York: Viking, 1926
MY HEART AND MY FLESH. New York: Viking, 1927
JINGLING IN THE WIND. New York: Viking, 1928
THE GREAT MEADOW. New York: Viking, 1930
A BURIED TREASURE. New York: Viking, 1931
HE SENT FORTH A RAVEN. New York: Viking, 1935
BLACK IS MY TRUELOVE'S HAIR. New York: Viking, 1938

KENNETH [LEWIS] ROBERTS (1885-1957)
ARUNDEL. Garden City: Doubleday, Doran, 1930
THE LIVELY LADY. Garden City: Doubleday, Doran, 1931
RABBLE IN ARMS. Garden City: Doubleday, Doran, 1933
CAPTAIN CAUTION. Garden City: Doubleday, Doran, 1934
NORTHWEST PASSAGE. Garden City: Doubleday, Doran, 1937
OLIVER WISWELL. Garden City: Doubleday, Doran, 1940
LYDIA BAILEY. Garden City: Doubleday, 1947
BOON ISLAND. Garden City: Doubleday, 1956

HENRIETTA RICHARDSON ROBERTSON: See HENRY HANDEL RICHARDSON

FREDERICK [WILLIAM SERAFINO AUSTIN LEWIS MARY] ROLFE, "BARON CORVO" (1860-1913)
HADRIAN THE SEVENTH.[1] London: Chatto & Windus, 1904
DON TARQUINIO. London: Chatto & Windus, 1905
DON RENATO. London: Griffiths, 1909 (Printed but not published). London: Chatto & Windus, 1963
THE WEIRD OF THE WANDERER (in collaboration with C. H. C. Pirie-Gordon; by "Prospero & Caliban"). London: Rider, 1912
THE DESIRE AND PURSUIT OF THE WHOLE.[1] London: Cassell, 1934
HUBERT'S ARTHUR (in collaboration with C. H. C. Pirie-Gordon; by "Prospero & Caliban"). London: Cassell, 1935
AMICO DI SANDRO (*fragment*). London: Privately printed, 1951
NICHOLAS CRABBE.[1] London: Chatto & Windus, 1958
[1]With IN HIS OWN IMAGE (London: Lane, 1901), a tetralogy

HENRY ROTH (1906-   )
CALL IT SLEEP. New York: Ballou, 1934

PHILIP [MILTON] ROTH (1933-   )
LETTING GO. New York: Random House, 1962

Sir EDWARD [CHARLES] SACKVILLE-WEST (1901-   )
PIANO QUINTET. London: Heinemann, 1925
THE RUIN. London: Heinemann, 1926
MANDRAKE OVER THE WATER-CARRIER. London: Heinemann, 1928
SIMPSON. London: Heinemann, 1931
THE SUN IN CAPRICORN. London: Heinemann, 1934

Hon. V[ICTORIA MARY] SACKVILLE-WEST (1892-1962)
HERITAGE. London: Collins, 1919
THE DRAGON IN SHALLOW WATERS. London: Collins, 1921
CHALLENGE. New York: Doran, 1923
GREY WETHERS. London: Heinemann, 1923
SEDUCERS IN ECUADOR. London: Hogarth, 1924
THE EDWARDIANS. London: Hogarth, 1930
ALL PASSION SPENT. London: Hogarth, 1931
FAMILY HISTORY. London: Hogarth, 1932
THE DARK ISLAND. London: Hogarth, 1934
GRAND CANYON. London: Joseph, 1942
DEVIL AT WESTEASE. Garden City: Doubleday, 1947
THE EASTER PARTY. London: Joseph, 1953
NO SIGNPOSTS IN THE SEA. London: Joseph, 1961

SAKI, i.e., H[ECTOR] H[UGH] MUNRO (1870-1916)
THE UNBEARABLE BASSINGTON. London: Lane, 1912
WHEN WILLIAM CAME. London: Lane, 1913

J[EROME] D[AVID] SALINGER (1919-   )
THE CATCHER IN THE RYE. Boston: Little, Brown, 1951

CARL [AUGUST] SANDBURG (1878-1967)
REMEMBRANCE ROCK. New York: Harcourt, Brace, 1948

WILLIAM SANSOM (1912-   )
THE BODY. London: Hogarth, 1949

THE FACE OF INNOCENCE. London: Hogarth, 1951
A BED OF ROSES. London: Hogarth, 1954
THE LOVING EYE. London: Hogarth, 1956
THE CAUTIOUS HEART. London: Hogarth, 1958
THE LAST HOURS OF SANDRA LEE. London: Hogarth, 1961
GOODBYE. London: Hogarth, 1966

GEORGE SANTAYANA(1863-1952)

THE LAST PURITAN. London: Constable, 1935. New York: Scribner, 1936

WILLIAM SAROYAN (1908-   )

THE HUMAN COMEDY. New York: Harcourt, Brace, 1943
THE ADVENTURES OF WESLEY JACKSON. New York: Harcourt, Brace, 1946
ROCK WAGRAM. Garden City: Doubleday, 1951
TRACY'S TIGER. Garden City: Doubleday, 1951
THE LAUGHING MATTER. Garden City: Doubleday, 1953
MAMA, I LOVE YOU. Boston: Atlantic-Little, Brown, 1956
PAPA, YOU'RE CRAZY. Boston: Atlantic-Little, Brown, 1957
BOYS AND GIRLS TOGETHER. New York: Harcourt, Brace & World, 1963
ONE DAY IN THE AFTERNOON OF THE WORLD. New York: Harcourt, Brace & World, 1964

MAY SARTON (1912-   )

THE SINGLE HOUND. Boston: Houghton Mifflin, 1938
THE BRIDGE OF YEARS. Garden City: Doubleday, 1946
SHADOW OF A MAN. New York: Rinehart, 1950
A SHOWER OF SUMMER DAYS. New York: Rinehart, 1952
FAITHFUL ARE THE WOUNDS. New York: Rinehart, 1955
THE FUR PERSON. New York: Rinehart, 1957
THE BIRTH OF A GRANDFATHER. New York: Rinehart, 1957
THE SMALL ROOM. New York: Norton, 1961
JOANNA AND ULYSSES. New York: Norton, 1963
MRS. STEVENS HEARS THE MERMAIDS SINGING. New York: Norton, 1965
MISS PICKTHORN AND MR. HARE. New York: Norton, 1966

SIEGFRIED [LORRAINE] SASSOON (1886-   )

MEMOIRS OF A FOX-HUNTING MAN[1] (Anonymous). London:

Faber & Gwyer, 1928. *James Tait Black Memorial Prize, 1929.*
Hawthornden Prize, 1929
MEMOIRS OF AN INFANTRY OFFICER.[1] London: Faber & Faber,
1930
SHERSTON'S PROGRESS.[1] London: Faber & Faber, 1936
[1]THE COMPLETE MEMOIRS OF GEORGE SHERSTON, London: Faber &
Faber, 1937; Garden City: Doubleday, Doran, 1937, under the title THE
MEMOIRS OF GEORGE SHERSTON

SYDNEY SCHIFF: See STEPHEN HUDSON

BUDD [WILSON] SCHULBERG (1914-)
WHAT MAKES SAMMY RUN? New York: Random House, 1941
THE HARDER THEY FALL. New York: Random House, 1947
THE DISENCHANTED. New York: Random House, 1950
WATERFRONT. New York: Random House, 1955

EVELYN SCOTT (1893-)
THE NARROW HOUSE. New York: Boni & Liveright, 1921
NARCISSUS. New York: Harcourt, Brace, 1922. London: Duck-
worth, 1922, under the title BEWILDERMENT
ESCAPADE. New York: Seltzer, 1923
THE GOLDEN DOOR. New York: Seltzer, 1925
MIGRATIONS. New York: Boni, 1927
THE WAVE. New York: Cape & Smith, 1929
BLUE RUM (by "Ernest Souza"). New York: Cape & Smith, 1930
A CALENDAR OF SIN. New York: Cape & Smith, 1931
EVA GAY. New York: Smith & Haas, 1933
BREATHE UPON THESE SLAIN. New York: Smith & Haas, 1934
BREAD AND A SWORD. New York: Scribner, 1937
THE SHADOW OF THE HAWK. New York: Scribner, 1941

J[OHN] D[ICK] SCOTT (1917-)
THE CELLAR. London: Pilot, 1947. New York: Pellegrini &
Cudahy, 1948, under the title BUY IT FOR A SONG
THE MARGIN. London: Pilot, 1949
THE WAY TO GLORY. London: Eyre & Spottiswoode, 1952
THE END OF AN OLD SONG. London: Eyre & Spottiswoode, 1954
THE PRETTY PENNY. London: Eyre & Spottiswoode, 1963

PAUL [MARK] SCOTT (1920-)
JOHNNIE SAHIB. London: Eyre & Spottiswoode, 1952

THE ALIEN SKY. London: Eyre & Spottiswoode, 1953. Garden
City: Doubleday, 1953, under the title SIX DAYS IN MARA-
PORE
A MALE CHILD. London: Eyre & Spottiswoode, 1956
THE MARK OF THE WARRIOR. London: Eyre & Spottiswoode,
1958
THE CHINESE LOVE PAVILION. London: Eyre & Spottiswoode,
1960. New York: Morrow, 1960, under the title THE LOVE
PAVILION
THE BIRDS OF PARADISE. London: Eyre & Spottiswoode, 1962
THE BENDER. London: Secker & Warburg, 1963
THE CORRIDA AT SAN FELIU. London: Secker & Warburg, 1964
THE JEWEL IN THE CROWN. London: Heinemann, 1966

JOHN SEDGES: See PEARL S[YDENSTRICKER] BUCK

ANNE DOUGLAS SEDGWICK (1873-1935)

THE DULL MISS ARCHINARD. New York: Scribner, 1898
THE CONFOUNDING OF CAMELIA. New York: Scribner, 1899
THE RESCUE. New York: Century, 1902
PATHS OF JUDGEMENT. New York: Century, 1904
THE SHADOW OF LIFE. New York: Century, 1906
A FOUNTAIN SEALED. New York: Century, 1907. London: Con-
stable, 1907, under the title VALERIE UPTON
AMABEL CHANNICE. New York: Century, 1908
FRANKLIN WINSLOW KANE. New York: Century, 1910. London:
Arnold, 1910, under the title FRANKLIN KANE
TANTE. New York: Century, 1911
THE ENCOUNTER. New York: Century, 1914
THE THIRD WINDOW. Boston: Houghton Mifflin, 1920
ADRIENNE TONER. London: Arnold, 1921. Boston: Houghton
Mifflin, 1922
THE LITTLE FRENCH GIRL. Boston: Houghton Mifflin, 1924
THE OLD COUNTESS. Boston: Houghton Mifflin, 1927
DARK HESTER. Boston: Houghton Mifflin, 1929
PHILIPPA. Boston: Houghton Mifflin, 1930

SAMUEL [DICKSON] SELVON (1924-   )

A BRIGHTER SUN. London: Wingate, 1952
AN ISLAND IS A WORLD. London: Wingate, 1955
THE LONELY LONDONERS. London: Wingate, 1956

TURN AGAIN TIGER. London: MacGibbon & Kee, 1958
I HEAR THUNDER. London: MacGibbon & Kee, 1963
THE HOUSING LARK. London: MacGibbon & Kee, 1965

MARY LEE SETTLE (-   )

THE LOVE EATERS. London: Heinemann, 1954. New York: Harper, [1955]
THE KISS OF KIN. London: Heinemann, 1955. New York: Harper, [1956]
O BEULAH LAND.[1] New York: Viking, 1956
KNOW NOTHING.[1] New York: Viking, 1960
FIGHT NIGHT ON A SWEET SATURDAY.[1] New York: Viking, 1964

[1] A trilogy

IRWIN SHAW (1913-   )

THE YOUNG LIONS. New York: Random House, 1948
THE TROUBLED AIR. New York: Random House, 1951
LUCY CROWN. New York: Random House, 1956
TWO WEEKS IN ANOTHER TOWN. New York: Random House, 1960
VOICES OF A SUMMER DAY. New York: Delacorte, 1965

ROBERT SHAW (1927-   )

THE HIDING PLACE. London: Chatto & Windus, 1959
THE SUN DOCTOR. London: Chatto & Windus, 1961. *Hawthornden Prize, 1962*
THE FLAG.[1] London: Chatto & Windus, 1965

[1] Vol. I of a projected trilogy, THE CURE OF SOULS

WILFRID [JOHN JOSEPH] SHEED (1930-   )

A MIDDLE CLASS EDUCATION. Boston: Houghton Mifflin, 1961
THE HACK. New York: Macmillan, 1963
SQUARE'S PROGRESS. New York: Farrar, Straus & Giroux, 1965
OFFICE POLITICS. New York: Farrar, Straus & Giroux, 1966

PATRIC SHONE: See JAMES HANLEY

ALAN SILLITOE (1928-   )

SATURDAY NIGHT AND SUNDAY MORNING. London: Allen, 1958. *Authors' Club First Novel Award, 1959*
THE GENERAL. London: Allen, 1960

KEY TO THE DOOR. London: Allen, 1961
THE DEATH OF WILLIAM POSTERS. London: Allen, 1965

EDITH SIMON (1917-   )

THE CHOSEN. London: Lane, 1940
BITING THE BLUE FINGER. London: Lane, 1942
WINGS DECEIVE. London: Lane, 1944
THE OTHER PASSION. London: Bodley Head, 1948
THE GOLDEN HAND. London: Cassell, 1952
THE PAST MASTERS. London: Cassell, 1953. New York: Putnam,
     1953, under the title THE HOUSE OF STRANGERS
THE TWELVE PICTURES. New York: Putnam, 1955. London:
     Cassell, 1956
THE SABLE COAT. London: Cassell, 1958
THE GREAT FORGERY. Boston: Little, Brown, 1961. London:
     Cassell, 1962

HELEN [DE GUERRY] SIMPSON (1897-1940)

ACQUITTAL. London: Heinemann, 1925
CUPS, WANDS AND SWORDS. London: Heinemann, 1927
ENTER SIR JOHN (in collaboration with Clemence Dane). London:
     Hodder & Stoughton, 1929
THE DESOLATE HOUSE. London: Heinemann, 1929. Garden
     City: Doubleday, Doran, 1930, under the title DESIRES AND
     DEVICES
PRINTER'S DEVIL (in collaboration with Clemence Dane).
     London: Hodder & Stoughton, 1930. New York: Cosmopolitan,
     1930, under the title AUTHOR UNKNOWN
'VANTAGE STRIKER. London: Heinemann, 1931. Garden City:
     Doubleday, Doran, 1931, under the title THE PRIME MINIS-
     TER IS DEAD
BOOMERANG. London: Heinemann, 1932. *James Tait Black Me-
     morial Prize, 1933*
RE-ENTER SIR JOHN (in collaboration with Clemence Dane).
     London: Hodder & Stoughton, 1932
THE WOMAN ON THE BEAST. London: Heinemann, 1933
SARABAND FOR DEAD LOVERS. London: Heinemann, 1935
THE FEMALE FELON. London: Dickson & Thompson, 1935
UNDER CAPRICORN. London: Heinemann, 1937
MAID NO MORE. London: Heinemann, 1940

ANDREW [ANNANDALE] SINCLAIR (1935-   )

THE BREAKING OF BUMBO. London: Faber & Faber, 1959

MY FRIEND JUDAS. London: Faber & Faber, 1959
THE PROJECT. London: Faber & Faber, 1960
THE HALLELUJAH BUM. London: Faber & Faber, 1963. New
    York: Atheneum, 1963, under the title TIIE PARADISE BUM
THE RAKER. London: Cape, 1964

MAY SINCLAIR (1870-1946)

AUDREY CRAVEN. Edinburgh: Blackwood, 1897
MR. AND MRS. NEVILL TYSON. Edinburgh: Blackwood, 1898.
    New York: Dodge, 1906, under the title THE TYSONS
THE DIVINE FIRE. London: Constable, 1904
THE HELPMATE. London: Constable, 1907
KITTY TAILLEUR. London: Constable, 1908. New York: Double-
    day, Page, 1908, under the title THE IMMORTAL MOMENT
THE CREATORS. London: Constable, 1910
THE COMBINED MAZE. London: Hutchinson, 1913
THE THREE SISTERS. London: Hutchinson, 1914
TASKER JEVONS. London: Hutchinson, 1916. New York: Mac-
    millan, 1916, under the title THE BELFRY
THE TREE OF HEAVEN. London: Cassell, 1917
MARY OLIVIER. London: Cassell, 1919
THE ROMANTIC. London: Collins, 1920
MR. WADDINGTON OF WYCK. London: Cassell, 1921
LIFE AND DEATH OF HARRIETT FREAN. London: Collins, 1922
ANNE SEVERN AND THE FIELDINGS. London: Hutchinson,
    1922
A CURE OF SOULS. London: Hutchinson, 1924
ARNOLD WATERLOW. London: Hutchinson, 1924
THE RECTOR OF WYCK. London: Hutchinson, 1925
FAR END. London: Hutchinson, 1926
THE ALLINGHAMS. London: Hutchinson, 1927
HISTORY OF ANTHONY WARING. London: Hutchinson, 1927

Note: SUPERSEDED (New York: Holt, 1906), often considered a separate
    novel, is actually excerpted from TWO SIDES OF A QUESTION (London:
    Constable, 1901).
    THE FLAW IN THE CRYSTAL (New York: Dutton, 1912) was published
    as a separate work in the U. S.; in England it was included in a
    collection, UNCANNY TALES (London: Hutchinson, 1923).

UPTON [BEALL] SINCLAIR [JR.] (1878-   )

SPRINGTIME AND HARVEST. New York: Sinclair, 1901. Reis-
    sued as KING MIDAS, New York: Funk & Wagnalls, 1901
THE JOURNAL OF ARTHUR STIRLING. New York: Appleton,
    1903

PRINCE HAGEN. Boston: Page, 1903
MANASSAS. New York: Macmillan, 1904. Reissued as THEIRS
    BE THE GUILT, New York: Twayne, 1959
A CAPTAIN OF INDUSTRY. Girard, Kansas: Appeal to Reason,
    1906
THE JUNGLE. New York: Doubleday, Page, 1906
THE METROPOLIS. New York: Moffat, Yard, 1908
THE MONEYCHANGERS. New York: Dodge, 1908
SAMUEL THE SEEKER. New York: Dodge, 1910
LOVE'S PILGRIMAGE. New York: Kennerley, 1911
DAMAGED GOODS. Philadelphia: Winston, 1913
SYLVIA. Philadelphia: Winston, 1913
SYLVIA'S MARRIAGE. Philadelphia: Winston, 1914
KING COAL. New York: Macmillan, 1917
JIMMIE HIGGINS. New York: Boni & Liveright, 1919
100%: THE STORY OF A PATRIOT. Pasadena, Calif.: Sinclair,
    1920. London: Laurie, 1921, under the title THE SPY
THEY CALL ME CARPENTER. Pasadena, Calif: Sinclair, 1922
THE MILLENIUM [pamphlet novel]. Girard, Kansas: Haldeman-
    Julius, 1924
OIL! New York: Boni, 1927
BOSTON. New York: Boni, 1928
MOUNTAIN CITY. New York: Boni, 1930
ROMAN HOLIDAY. New York: Farrar & Rinehart, 1931
THE WET PARADE. New York: Farrar & Rinehart, 1931
CO-OP. New York: Farrar & Rinehart, 1936
THE FLIVVER KING [pamphlet novel]. Pasadena, Calif.: Sinclair,
    1937
NO PASARÁN [pamphlet novel]. Pasadena, Calif.: Sinclair, 1937
LITTLE STEEL. New York: Farrar & Rinehart, 1938
OUR LADY. Emaus, Penn.: Rodale, 1938
WORLD'S END.[1] New York: Viking, 1940
BETWEEN TWO WORLDS.[1] New York: Viking, 1941
DRAGON'S TEETH.[1] New York: Viking, 1942. *Pulitzer Prize, 1943*
WIDE IS THE GATE.[1] New York: Viking, 1943
PRESIDENTIAL AGENT.[1] New York: Viking, 1944
DRAGON HARVEST.[1] New York: Viking, 1945
A WORLD TO WIN.[1] New York: Viking, 1946
PRESIDENTIAL MISSION.[1] New York: Viking, 1947
ONE CLEAR CALL.[1] New York: Viking, 1948
O SHEPHERD, SPEAK![1] New York: Viking, 1949
ANOTHER PAMELA. New York: Viking, 1950
THE RETURN OF LANNY BUDD.[1] New York: Viking, 1953

IT HAPPENED TO DIDYMUS. New York: Sagamore, 1958. London: Wingate, 1954, under the title WHAT DIDYMUS DID AFFECTIONATELY, EVE. New York: Twayne, 1961
[1]The Lanny Budd series

KHUSHWANT SINGH (1915-   )
TRAIN TO PAKISTAN. London: Chatto & Windus, 1956. New York: Grove, 1956, under the title MANO MAJRA
I SHALL NOT HEAR THE NIGHTINGALE. New York: Grove, 1959. London: Calder, 1961

JOHN SINJOHN: See JOHN GALSWORTHY

BETTY [WEHNER] SMITH (1904-   )
A TREE GROWS IN BROOKLYN. New York: Harper, 1943
TOMORROW WILL BE BETTER. New York: Harper, 1948
MAGGIE-NOW. New York: Harper, 1958
JOY IN THE MORNING. New York: Harper & Row, 1963

LILLIAN [EUGENIA] SMITH (1897-1966)
STRANGE FRUIT. New York: Reynal & Hitchcock, 1944
ONE HOUR. New York: Harcourt, Brace, 1959

Lord C[HARLES] P[ERCY] SNOW (1905-   )
DEATH UNDER SAIL. London: Heinemann, 1932
NEW LIVES FOR OLD. London: Gollancz, 1933
THE SEARCH. London: Gollancz, 1934
STRANGERS AND BROTHERS.[1] London: Faber & Faber, 1940
THE LIGHT AND THE DARK.[1] London: Faber & Faber, 1947
TIME OF HOPE.[1] London: Faber & Faber, 1949
THE MASTERS.[1] London: Macmillan, 1951. *James Tait Black Memorial Prize, 1955*
THE NEW MEN.[1] London: Macmillan, 1954. *James Tait Black Memorial Prize, 1955*
HOMECOMINGS.[1] London: Macmillan, 1956. New York: Scribner, 1956, under the title HOMECOMING
THE CONSCIENCE OF THE RICH.[1] London: Macmillan, 1958
THE AFFAIR.[1] London: Macmillan, 1960
CORRIDORS OF POWER.[1] London: Macmillan, 1964
[1]A sequence: STRANGERS AND BROTHERS

ERNEST SOUZA: See EVELYN SCOTT

MURIEL [SARAH] SPARK (1918-   )

THE COMFORTERS. London: Macmillan, 1957
ROBINSON. London: Macmillan, 1958
MEMENTO MORI. London: Macmillan, 1959
THE BALLAD OF PECKHAM RYE. London: Macmillan, 1960
THE BACHELORS. London: Macmillan, 1960
THE PRIME OF MISS JEAN BRODIE. London: Macmillan, 1961
THE GIRLS OF SLENDER MEANS. London: Macmillan, 1963
THE MANDELBAUM GATE. London: Macmillan, 1965. *James Tait Black Memorial Prize, 1966*

ELIZABETH SPENCER (1921-   )

FIRE IN THE MORNING. New York: Dodd, Mead, 1948
THIS CROOKED WAY. New York: Dodd, Mead, 1952
THE VOICE AT THE BACK DOOR. New York: McGraw-Hill, 1956. *Rosenthal Award, 1957*
THE LIGHT IN THE PIAZZA. New York: McGraw-Hill, 1960
KNIGHTS AND DRAGONS. New York: McGraw-Hill, 1965

DAVID [DEREK] STACTON (1925-   )

DOLORES. London: Faber & Faber, 1954
A FOX INSIDE. London: Faber & Faber, 1955
THE SELF-ENCHANTED. London: Faber & Faber, 1956
REMEMBER ME.[1] London: Faber & Faber, 1957
ON A BALCONY.[1] London: Faber & Faber, 1958. New York: London House & Maxwell, 1959
SEGAKI.[1] London: Faber & Faber, 1958. New York: Pantheon, 1959
WISH ME DEAD (by "David West"). London: Eyre & Spottiswoode, 1960
A SIGNAL VICTORY. London: Faber & Faber, 1960. New York: Pantheon, 1962
A DANCER IN DARKNESS. London: Faber & Faber, 1960. New York: Pantheon, 1962
THE JUDGES OF THE SECRET COURT. New York: Pantheon, 1961
TOM FOOL. London: Faber & Faber, 1962
OLD ACQUAINTANCE. London: Faber & Faber, 1962. New York: Putnam, 1964
SIR WILLIAM. New York: Putnam, 1963
KALIYUGA. London: Faber & Faber, 1965
PEOPLE OF THE BOOK. New York: Putnam, 1965

[1]A series: THE INVINCIBLE QUESTIONS

JEAN STAFFORD (1915-   )
BOSTON ADVENTURE. New York: Harcourt, Brace, 1944
THE MOUNTAIN LION. New York: Harcourt, Brace, 1947
THE CATHERINE WHEEL. New York: Harcourt, Brace, 1952

GEORGE STAIRS: See MARY [HUNTER] AUSTIN

CHRISTINA [ELLEN] STEAD (1902-   )
SEVEN POOR MEN OF SYDNEY. London: Davies, 1934
THE BEAUTIES AND FURIES. London: Davies, 1936
HOUSE OF ALL NATIONS. London: Davies, 1938
THE MAN WHO LOVED CHILDREN. New York: Simon & Schus-
    ter, 1940. London: Davies, 1941
FOR LOVE ALONE. New York: Harcourt, Brace, 1944. London:
    Davies, 1945
LETTY FOX, HER LUCK. New York: Harcourt, Brace, 1946.
    London: Davies, 1947
A LITTLE TEA, A LITTLE CHAT. New York: Harcourt, Brace,
    1948
THE PEOPLE WITH THE DOGS. Boston: Little, Brown, 1952
DARK PLACES OF THE HEART. New York: Holt, Rinehart &
    Winston, 1966

WALLACE [EARLE] STEGNER (1909-   )
REMEMBERING LAUGHTER. Boston: Little, Brown, 1937
THE POTTER'S HOUSE. Muscatine, Iowa: Prairie, 1938
ON A DARKLING PLAIN. New York: Harcourt, Brace, 1940
FIRE AND ICE. New York: Duell, Sloan & Pearce, 1941
THE BIG ROCK CANDY MOUNTAIN. New York: Duell, Sloan &
    Pearce, 1943
SECOND GROWTH. Boston: Houghton Mifflin, 1947
THE PREACHER AND THE SLAVE. Boston: Houghton Mifflin,
    1950
A SHOOTING STAR. New York: Viking, 1961

GERTRUDE STEIN (1874-1946)
THE MAKING OF AMERICANS. Paris: Contact Editions, 1925.
    New York: Boni, 1926
LUCY CHURCH AMIABLY. Paris: Plain Edition, 1930
IDA. New York: Random House, 1941

BLOOD ON THE DINING-ROOM FLOOR. Pawlet, Vt.: Banyan, 1948
THINGS AS THEY ARE. Pawlet, Vt.: Banyan, 1950
MRS. REYNOLDS. New Haven: Yale, 1952
A NOVEL OF THANK YOU. New Haven: Yale, 1958

JOHN [ERNST] STEINBECK (1902-   )
Nobel Prize for Literature, 1962
CUP OF GOLD. New York: McBride, 1929
THE PASTURES OF HEAVEN. New York: Brewer, Warren & Putnam, 1932
TO A GOD UNKNOWN. New York: Ballou, 1933
TORTILLA FLAT. New York: Covici-Friede, 1935
IN DUBIOUS BATTLE. New York: Covici-Friede, 1936
OF MICE AND MEN. New York: Covici-Friede, 1937
THE RED PONY. New York: Covici-Friede, 1937
THE GRAPES OF WRATH. New York: Viking, 1939. *Pulitzer Prize, 1940*
THE MOON IS DOWN. New York: Viking, 1942
CANNERY ROW. New York: Viking, 1945
THE WAYWARD BUS. New York: Viking, 1947
THE PEARL. New York: Viking, 1947
BURNING BRIGHT. New York: Viking, 1950
EAST OF EDEN. New York: Viking, 1952
SWEET THURSDAY. New York: Viking, 1954
THE SHORT REIGN OF PIPPIN IV. New York: Viking, 1957
THE WINTER OF OUR DISCONTENT. New York: Viking, 1961

JAMES STEPHENS (1882-1950)
THE CHARWOMAN'S DAUGHTER. London: Macmillan, 1912. Boston: Small, Maynard, 1912, under the title MARY, MARY
THE CROCK OF GOLD. London: Macmillan, 1912. *Polignac Prize, 1913*
THE DEMI-GODS. London: Macmillan, 1914
DEIRDRE. London: Macmillan, 1923
IN THE LAND OF YOUTH. London: Macmillan, 1924

DAVID STOREY (1933-   )
THIS SPORTING LIFE. London: Longmans, 1960
FLIGHT INTO CAMDEN. London: Longmans, 1960. *John Llewelyn Rhys Memorial Prize, 1961. Somerset Maugham Award, 1963*
RADCLIFFE. London: Longmans, 1963

T[HOMAS] S[IGISMUND] STRIBLING (1881-1965)

THE CRUISE OF THE DRY DOCK. Chicago: Reilly & Britton, 1917

BIRTHRIGHT. New York: Century, 1922

FOMBOMBO. New York: Century, 1923

RED SAND. New York: Harcourt, Brace, 1924

TEEFTALLOW. Garden City: Doubleday, Page, 1926

EAST IS EAST. New York: Allen, 1928

BRIGHT METAL. Garden City: Doubleday, Doran, 1928

STRANGE MOON. Garden City: Doubleday, Doran, 1929

BACKWATER. Garden City: Doubleday, Doran, 1930

THE FORGE.[1] Garden City: Doubleday, Doran, 1931

THE STORE.[1] Garden City: Doubleday, Doran, 1932. *Pulitzer Prize, 1933*

UNFINISHED CATHEDRAL.[1] Garden City: Doubleday, Doran, 1934

THE SOUND WAGON. Garden City: Doubleday, Doran, 1935

THESE BARS OF FLESH. Garden City: Doubleday, Doran, 1938

[1]A trilogy

L[EONARD] A[LFRED] G[EORGE] STRONG (1895-1958)

DEWER RIDES. London: Gollancz, 1929

THE JEALOUS GHOST. London: Gollancz, 1930

THE GARDEN. London: Gollancz, 1931

THE BROTHERS. London: Gollancz, 1932. New York: Knopf, 1932, under the title BROTHERS

SEA WALL. London: Gollancz, 1933

CORPORAL TUNE. London: Gollancz, 1934

THE SEVEN ARMS. London: Gollancz, 1935

THE LAST ENEMY. London: Gollancz, 1936

THE SWIFT SHADOW. London: Gollancz, 1937. New York: Knopf, 1937, under the title LAUGHTER IN THE WEST

THE OPEN SKY. London: Gollancz, 1939

THE BAY. London: Gollancz, 1941

SLOCOMBE DIES. London: Collins, 1942

THE UNPRACTISED HEART. London: Gollancz, 1942

ALL FALL DOWN. London: Collins, 1944

THE DIRECTOR. London: Methuen, 1944

OTHELLO'S OCCUPATION. London: Collins, 1945. Garden City: Doubleday, Doran, 1945, under the title MURDER PLAYS AN UGLY SCENE

TREVANNION. London: Methuen, 1948
WHICH I NEVER. London: Collins, 1950
THE HILL OF HOWTH. London: Methuen, 1953
DELIVERANCE. London: Methuen, 1955
TREASON IN THE EGG. London: Collins, 1958
LIGHT ABOVE THE LAKE. London: Methuen, 1958

JESSE [HILTON] STUART (1907-   )
TREES OF HEAVEN. New York: Dutton, 1940
TAPS FOR PRIVATE TUSSIE. New York: Dutton, 1943. London: Dobson, 1947, under the title HE'LL BE COMING DOWN THE MOUNTAIN
MONGREL METTLE. New York: Books, 1944
FORETASTE OF GLORY. New York: Dutton, 1946
HIE TO THE HUNTERS. New York: Whittlesey House, 1950
THE GOOD SPIRIT OF LAUREL RIDGE. New York: McGraw-Hill, 1953
DAUGHTER OF THE LEGEND. New York: McGraw-Hill, 1965

WILLIAM STYRON (1925-   )
LIE DOWN IN DARKNESS. Indianapolis: Bobbs-Merrill, 1951
THE LONG MARCH. New York: Random House, 1956
SET THIS HOUSE ON FIRE. New York: Random House, 1960

RUTH SUCKOW (1892-1960)
COUNTRY PEOPLE.[1] New York: Knopf, 1924
THE ODYSSEY OF A NICE GIRL. New York: Knopf, 1925
THE BONNEY FAMILY.[1] New York: Knopf, 1928
CORA. New York: Knopf, 1929
THE KRAMER GIRLS. New York: Knopf, 1930
THE FOLKS. New York: Farrar & Rinehart, 1934
NEW HOPE. New York: Farrar & Rinehart, 1942
THE JOHN WOOD CASE. New York: Viking, 1959
[1]Collected (with stories) in CARRY-OVER, New York: Farrar & Rinehart, 1936

WALTER [LAURENCE] SULLIVAN (1924-   )
SOJOURN OF A STRANGER. New York: Holt, 1957
THE LONG, LONG LOVE. New York: Holt, 1959

HARVEY SWADOS (1920-   )
OUT WENT THE CANDLE. New York: Viking, 1955

FALSE COIN. Boston: Atlantic-Little, Brown, 1959
THE WILL. Cleveland: World, 1963

FRANK [ARTHUR] SWINNERTON (1884-   )

THE MERRY HEART. London: Chatto & Windus, 1909
THE YOUNG IDEA. London: Chatto & Windus, 1910
THE CASEMENT. London: Chatto & Windus, 1911
THE HAPPY FAMILY. London: Methuen, 1912
ON THE STAIRCASE. London: Methuen, 1914
THE CHASTE WIFE. London: Secker, 1916
NOCTURNE. London: Secker, 1917
SHOPS AND HOUSES. London: Methuen, 1918
SEPTEMBER. London: Methuen, 1919
COQUETTE. London: Methuen, 1921
THE THREE LOVERS. London: Methuen, 1922
YOUNG FELIX. London: Hutchinson, 1923
THE ELDER SISTER. London: Hutchinson, 1925
SUMMER STORM. London: Hutchinson, 1926
A BROOD OF DUCKLINGS. London: Hutchinson, 1928
SKETCH OF A SINNER. London: Hutchinson, 1929
THE GEORGIAN HOUSE. London: Hutchinson, 1932
ELIZABETH. London: Hutchinson, 1934
HARVEST COMEDY. London: Hutchinson, 1937
THE TWO WIVES. London: Hutchinson, 1939
THE FORTUNATE LADY. London: Hutchinson, 1941
THANKLESS CHILD. London: Hutchinson, 1942
A WOMAN IN SUNSHINE. London: Hutchinson, 1944
ENGLISH MAIDEN. London: Hutchinson, 1946
FAITHFUL COMPANY. London: Hutchinson, 1948
THE DOCTOR'S WIFE COMES TO STAY. London: Hutchinson,
    1949
A FLOWER FOR CATHERINE. London: Hutchinson, 1950
MASTER JIM PROBITY. London: Hutchinson, 1952. Garden City:
    Doubleday, 1953, under the title AN AFFAIR OF LOVE
A MONTH IN GORDON SQUARE. London: Hutchinson, 1953
THE SUMNER INTRIGUE. London: Hutchinson, 1955
THE WOMAN FROM SICILY. London: Hutchinson, 1957
A TIGRESS IN PROTHERO. London: Hutchinson, 1959. Garden
    City: Doubleday, 1959, under the title A TIGRESS IN THE
    VILLAGE
THE GRACE DIVORCE. London: Hutchinson, 1960
DEATH OF A HIGHBROW. London: Hutchinson, 1961
QUADRILLE. London: Hutchinson, 1965
SANCTUARY. London: Hutchinson, 1966

[NEWTON] BOOTH TARKINGTON (1869-1946)

Gold Medal for Fiction, National Institute of Arts and Letters, 1933. Howells Medal, American Academy of Arts and Letters, 1945

THE GENTLEMAN FROM INDIANA. New York: Doubleday & McClure, 1899
MONSIEUR BEAUCAIRE. New York: McClure, Phillips, 1900
THE TWO VANREVELS. New York: McClure, Phillips, 1902
CHERRY. New York: Harper, 1903
THE BEAUTIFUL LADY. New York: McClure, Phillips, 1905
THE CONQUEST OF CANAAN. New York: Harper, 1905
HIS OWN PEOPLE. New York: Doubleday, Page, 1907
THE GUEST OF QUESNAY. New York: McClure, 1908
BEASLEY'S CHRISTMAS PARTY. New York: Harper, 1909
BEAUTY AND THE JACOBIN. New York: Harper, 1912
THE FLIRT. Garden City: Doubleday, Page, 1913
PENROD.[1] Garden City: Doubleday, Page, 1914
THE TURMOIL.[2] New York: Harper, 1915
SEVENTEEN. New York: Harper, 1916
PENROD AND SAM.[1] Garden City: Doubleday, Page, 1916
THE MAGNIFICENT AMBERSONS.[2] Garden City: Doubleday, Page, 1918. *Pulitzer Prize, 1919*
RAMSEY MILHOLLAND. Garden City: Doubleday, Page, 1919
ALICE ADAMS. Garden City: Doubleday, Page, 1921. *Pulitzer Prize, 1922*
HARLEQUIN AND COLUMBINE. Garden City: Doubleday, Page, 1921
GENTLE JULIA. Garden City: Doubleday, Page, 1922
THE MIDLANDER.[2] Garden City: Doubleday, Page, 1924
WOMEN. Garden City: Doubleday, Page, 1925
THE PLUTOCRAT. Garden City: Doubleday, Page, 1927
CLAIRE AMBLER. Garden City: Doubleday, Doran, 1928
YOUNG MRS. GREELEY. Garden City: Doubleday, Doran, 1929
PENROD JASHBER.[1] Garden City: Doubleday, Doran, 1929
MIRTHFUL HAVEN. Garden City: Doubleday, Doran, 1930
MARY'S NECK. Garden City: Doubleday, Doran, 1932
WANTON MALLY. Garden City: Doubleday, Doran, 1932
PRESENTING LILY MARS. Garden City: Doubleday, Doran, 1933
LITTLE ORVIE. Garden City: Doubleday, Doran, 1934
THE LORENZO BUNCH. Garden City: Doubleday, Doran, 1936
RUMBIN GALLERIES. Garden City: Doubleday, Doran, 1937
THE HERITAGE OF HATCHER IDE. Garden City: Doubleday, Doran, 1941

THE FIGHTING LITTLES. Garden City: Doubleday, Doran, 1941
KATE FENNIGATE. Garden City: Doubleday, Doran, 1943
IMAGE OF JOSEPHINE. Garden City: Doubleday, Doran, 1945
THE SHOW PIECE (unfinished). Garden City: Doubleday, 1947
[1]Collected as PENROD: HIS COMPLETE STORY, Garden City: Doubleday, Doran, 1931
[2]A trilogy: GROWTH, Garden City: Doubleday, Page, 1927 (title of THE MIDLANDER changed to NATIONAL AVENUE)

[JOHN ORLEY] ALLEN TATE (1899-   )
THE FATHERS. New York: Putnam, 1938

ELIZABETH [COLES] TAYLOR (1912-   )
AT MRS. LIPPINCOTE'S London: Davies, 1945
PALLADIAN. London: Davies, 1946
A VIEW OF THE HARBOUR. London: Davies, 1947
A WREATH OF ROSES. London: Davies, 1949
A GAME OF HIDE-AND-SEEK. London: Davies, 1951
THE SLEEPING BEAUTY. London: Davies, 1953
ANGEL. London: Davies, 1957
IN A SUMMER SEASON. London: Davies, 1961
THE SOUL OF KINDNESS. London: Chatto & Windus, 1964

KAMALA PURNAIYA TAYLOR: See KAMALA MARKANDAYA

PETER [HILLSMAN] TAYLOR (1917-   )
A WOMAN OF MEANS. New York: Harcourt, Brace, 1950

ROBERT LEWIS TAYLOR (1912-   )
ADRIFT IN A BONEYARD. Garden City: Doubleday, 1947
PROFESSOR FODORSKI. Garden City: Doubleday, 1950
THE BRIGHT SANDS. Garden City: Doubleday, 1954
THE TRAVELS OF JAIMIE McPHEETERS. Garden City: Doubleday, 1958. Pulitzer Prize, 1959
A JOURNEY TO MATECUMBE. New York: McGraw-Hill, 1961
TWO ROADS TO GUADELUPÉ. Garden City: Doubleday, 1964

J[OHN] R[ONALD] R[ENEL] TOLKIEN (1892-   )
THE HOBBIT. London: Allen & Unwin, 1937
THE FELLOWSHIP OF THE RING.[1] London: Allen & Unwin, 1954

THE TWO TOWERS.[1] London: Allen & Unwin, 1954
THE RETURN OF THE KING.[1] London: Allen & Unwin, 1955
[1] A trilogy: THE LORD OF THE RINGS

H[ENRY] M[AJOR] TOMLINSON (1873-1958)

GALLIONS REACH. London: Heinemann, 1927. *Femina-Vie Heu-reuse Prize, 1929*
ALL OUR YESTERDAYS. London: Heinemann, 1930
THE SNOWS OF HELICON. London: Heinemann, 1933
ALL HANDS! London: Heinemann, 1937. New York: Harper, 1937, under the title PIPE ALL HANDS
THE DAY BEFORE. New York: Putnam, 1939. London: Heinemann, 1940
MORNING LIGHT. London: Hodder & Stoughton, 1946
THE TRUMPET SHALL SOUND. London: Hodder & Stoughton, 1957

[THEODORE] PHILIP TOYNBEE (1916-   )

THE SAVAGE DAYS. London: Hamilton, 1937
SCHOOL IN PRIVATE. London: Putnam, 1941
THE BARRICADES. London: Putnam, 1943
TEA WITH MRS. GOODMAN. London: MacGibbon & Kee, 1947. Garden City: Doubleday, 1947, under the title PROTHALA-MIUM
THE GARDEN TO THE SEA. London: MacGibbon & Kee, 1953
PANTALOON.[1] London: Chatto & Windus, 1961

[1] Vol. I, in prose and verse, of a series; its sequels (London: Chatto & Windus), TWO BROTHERS (1964) and A LEARNED CITY (1966), are in verse.

HONOR [LILBUSH WINGFIELD] TRACY (1915-   )

THE DESERTERS. London: Methuen, 1954
THE STRAIGHT AND NARROW PATH. London: Methuen, 1956
THE PROSPECTS ARE PLEASING. London: Methuen, 1958
A NUMBER OF THINGS. London: Methuen, 1960
A SEASON OF MISTS. London: Methuen, 1961
THE FIRST DAY OF FRIDAY. London: Methuen, 1963
MEN AT WORK. London: Methuen, 1966

HENRY [WILLIAM] TREECE (1911-1966)

THE DARK ISLAND. London: Gollancz, 1952
THE REBELS. London: Gollancz, 1953

THE GREAT CAPTAINS. London: Bodley Head, 1956
THE GOLDEN STRANGERS. London: Bodley Head, 1956
RED QUEEN, WHITE QUEEN. London: Bodley Head, 1958
A FIGHTING MAN. London: Bodley Head, 1960. New York:
    Random House, 1959, under the title THE MASTER OF
    BADGER'S HALL
JASON.[1] London: Bodley Head, 1961
ELECTRA.[1] London: Bodley Head, 1963. New York: Random
    House, 1963, under the title AMBER PRINCESS
OEDIPUS.[1] London: Bodley Head, 1964. New York: Random
    House, 1965, under the title THE EAGLE KING
THE GREEN MAN. London: Bodley Head, 1966
[1]A trilogy

GLEN TREVOR: See JAMES HILTON

WILLIAM TREVOR [COX] (1928-   )
A STANDARD OF BEHAVIOUR. London: Hutchinson, 1958
THE OLD BOYS. London: Bodley Head, 1964. *Hawthornden Prize,
    1965*
THE BOARDING-HOUSE. London: Bodley Head, 1965
THE LOVE DEPARTMENT. London: Bodley Head, 1966

LIONEL TRILLING (1905-   )
THE MIDDLE OF THE JOURNEY. New York: Viking, 1947

[JOHN FRANCIS] FRANK TUOHY (1925-   )
THE ANIMAL GAME. London: Macmillan, 1957
THE WARM NIGHTS OF JANUARY. London: Macmillan, 1960
THE ICE SAINTS. London: Macmillan, 1964. *James Tait Black
    Memorial Prize, 1965. Geoffrey Faber Memorial Prize, 1965*

AMOS TUTUOLA (1920-   )
THE PALM-WINE DRINKARD. London: Faber & Faber, 1952
MY LIFE IN THE BUSH OF GHOSTS. London: Faber & Faber,
    1954
SIMBI AND THE SATYR OF THE DARK JUNGLE. London:
    Faber & Faber, 1955
THE FEATHER WOMAN OF THE JUNGLE. London: Faber &
    Faber, 1962

JOHN [HOYER] UPDIKE (1932-   )

THE POORHOUSE FAIR. New York: Knopf, 1959. *Rosenthal Award, 1960*
RABBIT, RUN. New York: Knopf, 1960
THE CENTAUR. New York: Knopf, 1963. *National Book Award, 1964*
OF THE FARM. New York: Knopf, 1965

CARL VAN VECHTEN (1880-1964)

PETER WHIFFLE. New York: Knopf, 1922
THE BLIND BOW-BOY. New York: Knopf, 1923
THE TATTOOED COUNTESS. New York: Knopf, 1924
FIRECRACKERS. New York: Knopf, 1925
NIGGER HEAVEN. New York: Knopf, 1926
SPIDER BOY. New York: Knopf, 1928
PARTIES. New York: Knopf, 1930

GORE VIDAL (1925-   )

WILLIWAW. New York: Dutton, 1946
IN A YELLOW WOOD. New York: Dutton, 1947
THE CITY AND THE PILLAR. New York: Dutton, 1948
THE SEASON OF COMFORT. New York: Dutton, 1949
A SEARCH FOR THE KING. New York: Dutton, 1950
DARK GREEN, BRIGHT RED. New York: Dutton, 1950
THE JUDGMENT OF PARIS. New York: Dutton, 1952
DEATH IN THE FIFTH POSITION (by "Edgar Box"). New York: Dutton, 1952
DEATH BEFORE BEDTIME (by "Edgar Box"). New York: Dutton, 1953
MESSIAH. New York: Dutton, 1954
DEATH LIKES IT HOT (by "Edgar Box"). New York: Dutton, 1954
JULIAN. Boston: Little, Brown, 1964

HELEN [JANE] WADDELL (1889-   )

PETER ABELARD. London: Constable, 1933

JOHN [BARRINGTON] WAIN (1925-   )

HURRY ON DOWN. London: Secker & Warburg, 1953. New York: Knopf, 1954, under the title BORN IN CAPTIVITY
LIVING IN THE PRESENT. London: Secker & Warburg, 1955
THE CONTENDERS. London: Macmillan, 1958

A TRAVELLING WOMAN. London: Macmillan, 1959
STRIKE THE FATHER DEAD. London: Macmillan, 1962
THE YOUNG VISITORS. London: Macmillan, 1965

EDWARD LEWIS WALLANT (1926-1962)
THE HUMAN SEASON. New York: Harcourt, Brace, 1960
THE PAWNBROKER. New York: Harcourt, Brace & World, 1961
THE TENANTS OF MOONBLOOM. New York: Harcourt, Brace & World, 1963
THE CHILDREN AT THE GATE. New York: Harcourt, Brace & World, 1964

Sir HUGH [SEYMOUR] WALPOLE (1884-1941)
THE WOODEN HORSE. London: Smith, Elder, 1909
MARADICK AT FORTY. London: Smith, Elder, 1910
MR. PERRIN AND MR. TRAILL. London: Mills & Boon, 1911. New York: Doran, 1911, under the title THE GODS AND MR. PERRIN
THE PRELUDE TO ADVENTURE. London: Mills & Boon, 1912
FORTITUDE. London: Secker, 1913
THE DUCHESS OF WREXE. London: Secker, 1914
THE DARK FOREST. London: Secker, 1916
THE GREEN MIRROR. London: Macmillan, 1918
THE SECRET CITY. London: Macmillan, 1919. *James Tait Black Memorial Prize, 1920*
JEREMY. London: Cassell, 1919
THE CAPTIVES. London: Macmillan, 1920
THE YOUNG ENCHANTED. London: Macmillan, 1921
THE CATHEDRAL. London: Macmillan, 1922
JEREMY AND HAMLET. London: Cassell, 1923
THE OLD LADIES. London: Macmillan, 1924
PORTRAIT OF A MAN WITH RED HAIR. London: Macmillan, 1925
HARMER JOHN. London: Macmillan, 1926
JEREMY AT CRALE. London: Cassell, 1927
WINTERSMOON. London: Macmillan, 1928
FARTHING HALL (in collaboration with J. B. Priestley). London: Macmillan, 1929
HANS FROST. London: Macmillan, 1929
ROGUE HERRIES.[1] London: Macmillan, 1930
ABOVE THE DARK CIRCUS. London: Macmillan, 1931. Garden City: Doubleday, Doran, 1931, under the title ABOVE THE DARK TUMULT

JUDITH PARIS.[1] London: Macmillan, 1931
THE FORTRESS.[1] London: Macmillan, 1932
VANESSA.[1] London: Macmillan, 1933
CAPTAIN NICHOLAS. London: Macmillan, 1934
THE INQUISITOR. London: Macmillan, 1935
A PRAYER FOR MY SON. London: Macmillan, 1936
JOHN CORNELIUS. London: Macmillan, 1937
THE JOYFUL DELANEYS. London: Macmillan, 1938
THE SEA TOWER. London: Macmillan, 1939
THE BRIGHT PAVILIONS. London: Macmillan, 1940
THE BLIND MAN'S HOUSE. London: Macmillan, 1941
THE KILLER AND THE SLAIN. London: Macmillan, 1942
KATHERINE CHRISTIAN (*unfinished*). London: Macmillan, 1944
[1]A tetralogy: THE HERRIES CHRONICLE, London: Macmillan, 1939

REX WARNER (1905-   )
THE WILD GOOSE CHASE. London: Boriswood, 1937
THE PROFESSOR. London: Boriswood, 1938
THE AERODROME. London: Lane, 1941
WHY WAS I KILLED? London: Lane, 1943. Philadelphia: Lip-
     pincott, 1944, under the title RETURN OF THE TRAVELLER
MEN OF STONES. London: Lane, 1949
ESCAPADE. London: Lane, 1953
THE YOUNG CAESAR. London: Collins, 1958
IMPERIAL CAESAR. London: Collins, 1960. *James Tait Black
     Memorial Prize, 1961*
PERICLES THE ATHENIAN. London: Collins, 1963

SYLVIA TOWNSEND WARNER (1893-   )
LOLLY WILLOWES. London: Chatto & Windus, 1926
MR. FORTUNE'S MAGGOT. London: Chatto & Windus, 1927
THE TRUE HEART. London: Chatto & Windus, 1929
SUMMER WILL SHOW. London: Chatto & Windus, 1936
AFTER THE DEATH OF DON JUAN. London: Chatto & Windus,
     1938
THE CORNER THAT HELD THEM. London: Chatto & Windus,
     1948
THE FLINT ANCHOR. London: Chatto & Windus, 1954

ROBERT PENN WARREN (1905-   )
NIGHT RIDER. Boston: Houghton Mifflin, 1939
AT HEAVEN'S GATE. New York: Harcourt, Brace, 1943
ALL THE KING'S MEN. New York: Harcourt, Brace, 1946. *Pulitzer
     Prize, 1947*

WORLD ENOUGH AND TIME. New York: Random House, 1950
BAND OF ANGELS. New York: Random House, 1955
THE CAVE. New York: Random House, 1959
WILDERNESS. New York: Random House, 1961
FLOOD. New York: Random House, 1964

KEITH WATERHOUSE (1929-   )
THERE IS A HAPPY LAND. London: Joseph, 1957
BILLY LIAR. London: Joseph, 1959
JUBB. London: Joseph, 1963

[ALEXANDER] ALEC [RABAN] WAUGH (1898-   )
THE LOOM OF YOUTH. London: Richards, 1917
THE LONELY UNICORN. London: Richards, 1922. New York: Macmillan, 1922, under the title RONALD WHATELY
CARD CASTLE. London: Richards, 1924
KEPT. London: Richards, 1925
LOVE IN THESE DAYS. London: Chapman & Hall, 1926
NOR MANY WATERS. London: Chapman & Hall, 1928. Garden City: Doubleday, Doran, 1929, under the title PORTRAIT OF A CELIBATE
THREE SCORE AND TEN. London: Chapman & Hall, 1929
". . . 'SIR,' SHE SAID". London: Chapman & Hall, 1930. New York: Farrar & Rinehart, 1930, under the title "SIR!" SHE SAID
SO LOVERS DREAM. London: Cassell, 1931. New York: Farrar & Rinehart, 1932, under the title THAT AMERICAN WOMAN
LEAP BEFORE YOU LOOK. London: Benn, 1932
NO QUARTER. London: Cassell, 1932. New York: Farrar & Rinehart, 1932, under the title TROPIC SEED
WHEELS WITHIN WHEELS. London: Cassell, 1933. New York: Farrar & Rinehart, 1933, under the title THE GOLDEN RIPPLE
PLAYING WITH FIRE. London: Benn, 1933
THE BALLIOLS. London: Cassell, 1934
JILL SOMERSET. London: Cassell, 1936
GOING THEIR OWN WAYS. London: Cassell, 1938
NO TRUCE WITH TIME. London: Cassell, 1941
UNCLOUDED SUMMER. London: Cassell, 1948
GUY RENTON. New York: Farrar, Straus & Young, 1952. London: Cassell, 1953
ISLAND IN THE SUN. London: Cassell, 1956
FUEL FOR THE FLAME. London: Cassell, 1960
THE MULE ON THE MINARET. London: Cassell, 1965

EVELYN [ARTHUR ST. JOHN] WAUGH, C.Litt. (1903-1966)

DECLINE AND FALL. London: Chapman & Hall, 1928
VILE BODIES. London: Chapman & Hall, 1930
BLACK MISCHIEF. London: Chapman & Hall, 1932
A HANDFUL OF DUST. London: Chapman & Hall, 1934
SCOOP. London: Chapman & Hall, 1938
PUT OUT MORE FLAGS. London: Chapman & Hall, 1942
WORK SUSPENDED (*fragment*). London: Chapman & Hall, 1942
BRIDESHEAD REVISITED. London: Chapman & Hall, 1945
SCOTT-KING'S MODERN EUROPE. London: Chapman & Hall, 1947
THE LOVED ONE. London: Chapman & Hall, 1948
HELENA. London: Chapman & Hall, 1950
MEN AT ARMS.[1] London: Chapman & Hall, 1952. *James Tait Black Memorial Prize, 1953*
LOVE AMONG THE RUINS. London: Chapman & Hall, 1953
OFFICERS AND GENTLEMEN.[1] London: Chapman & Hall, 1955
THE ORDEAL OF GILBERT PINFOLD. London: Chapman & Hall, 1957
UNCONDITIONAL SURRENDER.[1] London: Chapman & Hall, 1961. Boston: Little, Brown, 1962, under the title THE END OF THE BATTLE
BASIL SEAL RIDES AGAIN. London: Chapman & Hall, 1963
[1]A trilogy: SWORD OF HONOUR, London: Chapman & Hall, 1965

MARY [GLADYS MEREDITH] WEBB (1883-1927)

THE GOLDEN ARROW. London: Constable, 1916
GONE TO EARTH. London: Constable, 1917
THE HOUSE IN DORMER FOREST. London: Hutchinson, 1920
SEVEN FOR A SECRET. London: Hutchinson, 1922
PRECIOUS BANE. London: Cape, 1924. *Femina-Vie Heureuse Prize, 1926*
ARMOUR WHEREIN HE TRUSTED (*unfinished*). London: Cape, 1929

NATHAN WALLENSTEIN WEINSTEIN: See NATHANAEL WEST

[MAURICE] DENTON WELCH (1915-1948)

MAIDEN VOYAGE. London: Routledge, 1943
IN YOUTH IS PLEASURE. London: Routledge, 1944

A VOICE THROUGH A CLOUD (*unfinished*). London: Lehmann, 1950

H[ERBERT] G[EORGE] WELLS (1866-1946)
THE TIME MACHINE. London: Heinemann, 1895
THE WONDERFUL VISIT. London: Dent, 1895
THE ISLAND OF DOCTOR MOREAU. London: Heinemann, 1896
THE WHEELS OF CHANCE. London: Dent, 1896
THE INVISIBLE MAN. London: Pearson, 1897
THE WAR OF THE WORLDS. London: Heinemann, 1898
WHEN THE SLEEPER WAKES. London: Harper, 1899. Reissued
    as THE SLEEPER AWAKES, London: Nelson, 1910
LOVE AND MR. LEWISHAM. London: Harper, 1900
THE FIRST MEN IN THE MOON. London: Newnes, 1901
THE SEA LADY. London: Methuen, 1902
THE FOOD OF THE GODS. London: Macmillan, 1904
KIPPS. London: Macmillan, 1905
IN THE DAYS OF THE COMET. London: Macmillan, 1906
THE WAR IN THE AIR. London: Bell, 1908
TONO-BUNGAY. London: Macmillan, 1909
ANN VERONICA. London: Unwin, 1909
THE HISTORY OF MR. POLLY. London: Nelson, 1910
THE NEW MACHIAVELLI. London: Lane, 1911
MARRIAGE. London: Macmillan, 1912
THE PASSIONATE FRIENDS. London: Macmillan, 1913
THE WORLD SET FREE. London: Macmillan, 1914
THE WIFE OF SIR ISAAC HARMAN. London: Macmillan, 1914
BEALBY. London: Methuen, 1915
THE RESEARCH MAGNIFICENT. London: Macmillan, 1915
MR. BRITLING SEES IT THROUGH. London: Cassell, 1916
THE SOUL OF A BISHOP. London: Cassell, 1917
JOAN AND PETER. London: Cassell, 1918
THE UNDYING FIRE. London: Cassell, 1919
THE SECRET PLACES OF THE HEART. London: Cassell, 1922
MEN LIKE GODS. London: Cassell, 1923
THE DREAM. London: Cape, 1924
CHRISTINA ALBERTA'S FATHER. London: Cape, 1925
THE WORLD OF WILLIAM CLISSOLD. London: Benn, 1926
MEANWHILE. London: Benn, 1927
MR. BLETTSWORTHY ON RAMPOLE ISLAND. London: Benn, 1928
THE KING WHO WAS A KING. London: Benn, 1929
THE AUTOCRACY OF MR. PARHAM. London: Heinemann, 1930
THE BULPINGTON OF BLUP. London: Hutchinson, 1933

THE SHAPE OF THINGS TO COME. London: Hutchinson, 1933
THE CROQUET PLAYER. London: Chatto & Windus, 1936
STAR-BEGOTTEN. London: Chatto & Windus, 1937
BRYNHILD. London: Methuen, 1937
THE CAMFORD VISITATION. London: Methuen, 1937
THE BROTHERS. London: Chatto & Windus, 1938
APROPOS OF DOLORES. London: Cape, 1938
THE HOLY TERROR. London: Joseph, 1939
ALL ABOARD FOR ARARAT. London: Secker & Warburg, 1940
BABES IN THE DARKLING WOOD. London: Secker & Warburg, 1940
YOU CAN'T BE TOO CAREFUL. London: Secker & Warburg, 1941

EUDORA WELTY (1909-   )

Howells Medal, American Academy of Arts and Letters, 1955
THE ROBBER BRIDEGROOM. Garden City: Doubleday, Doran, 1942
DELTA WEDDING. New York: Harcourt, Brace, 1946
THE PONDER HEART. New York: Harcourt, Brace, 1954. *Howells Medal, 1955*

GLENWAY WESCOTT (1901-   )

THE APPLE OF THE EYE. New York: Dial, 1924
THE GRANDMOTHERS. New York: Harper, 1927. London: Butterworth, 1927, under the title A FAMILY PORTRAIT. *Harper Prize, 1927*
THE BABE'S BED. Paris: Harrison, 1930
THE PILGRIM HAWK. New York: Harper, 1940
APARTMENT IN ATHENS. New York: Harper, 1945. London: Hamilton, 1945, under the title HOUSEHOLD IN ATHENS

ANTHONY [PANTHER] WEST (1914-   )

THE VINTAGE. Boston: Houghton Mifflin, 1950. London: Eyre & Spottiswoode, 1949, under the title ON A DARK NIGHT
ANOTHER KIND. London: Eyre & Spottiswoode, 1951. Boston: Houghton Mifflin, 1952
HERITAGE. New York: Random House, 1955
THE TREND IS UP. New York: Random House, 1960

DAVID WEST: See DAVID [DEREK] STACTON

JESSAMYN WEST (1907-   )

THE WITCH DIGGERS. New York: Harcourt, Brace, 1951
SOUTH OF THE ANGELS. New York: Harcourt, Brace, 1960
A MATTER OF TIME. New York: Harcourt, Brace & World, 1966

Note: THE FRIENDLY PERSUASION (New York: Harcourt, Brace, 1945)
and CRESS DELAHANTY (New York: Harcourt, Brace, 1953), though
generally regarded as novels, are, according to the author, collections of
stories.

MORRIS [LANGLO] WEST (1916-   )

GALLOWS ON THE SAND. Sydney: Angus & Robertson, 1956
KUNDU. Sydney: Angus & Robertson, 1957
THE BIG STORY. London: Heinemann, 1957. New York: Morrow,
    1957, under the title THE CROOKED ROAD
McCREARY MOVES IN (by "Michael East"). London: Heine-
    mann, 1958
SECOND VICTORY. London: Heinemann, 1958. New York: Mor-
    row, 1958, under the title BACKLASH
THE DEVIL'S ADVOCATE. London: Heinemann, 1959. *James
    Tait Black Memorial Prize, 1960. Heinemann Award, 1960*
NAKED COUNTRY (by "Michael East"). London: Heinemann,
    1960
DAUGHTER OF SILENCE. London: Heinemann, 1961
THE SHOES OF THE FISHERMAN. London: Heinemann, 1963
THE AMBASSADOR. London: Heinemann, 1965

NATHANAEL WEST, i.e. NATHAN
WALLENSTEIN WEINSTEIN (1902-1940)

THE DREAM LIFE OF BALSO SNELL. New York: Moss &
    Kamin, 1931
MISS LONELYHEARTS. New York: Liveright, 1933
A COOL MILLION. New York: Covici-Friede, 1934
THE DAY OF THE LOCUST. New York: Random House, 1939

Dame REBECCA WEST, i.e. CICILY ISABEL
FAIRFIELD ANDREWS (1892-   )

THE RETURN OF THE SOLDIER. London: Nisbet, 1918
THE JUDGE. London: Hutchinson, 1922
HARRIET HUME. London: Hutchinson, 1929
WAR NURSE (by "Corinne Andrews"). New York: Cosmopolitan,
    1930
THE THINKING REED. London: Hutchinson, 1936

THE FOUNTAIN OVERFLOWS. New York: Viking, 1956. London: Macmillan, 1957
THE BIRDS FALL DOWN. London: Macmillan, 1966

EDITH [NEWBOLD JONES] WHARTON (1862-1937)

Gold Medal for Fiction, National Institute of Arts and Letters, 1924
THE TOUCHSTONE. New York: Scribner, 1900. London: Murray, 1900, under the title A GIFT FROM THE GRAVE
THE VALLEY OF DECISION. New York: Scribner, 1902
SANCTUARY. New York: Scribner, 1903
THE HOUSE OF MIRTH. New York: Scribner, 1905
MADAME DE TREYMES. New York: Scribner, 1907
THE FRUIT OF THE TREE. New York: Scribner, 1907
ETHAN FROME. New York: Scribner, 1911
THE REEF. New York: Appleton, 1912
THE CUSTOM OF THE COUNTRY. New York: Scribner, 1913
SUMMER. New York: Appleton, 1917
THE MARNE. New York: Appleton, 1918
THE AGE OF INNOCENCE. New York: Appleton, 1920. *Pulitzer Prize, 1921*
THE GLIMPSES OF THE MOON. New York: Appleton, 1922
A SON AT THE FRONT. New York: Scribner, 1923
OLD NEW YORK:
    FALSE DAWN
    THE OLD MAID
    THE SPARK
    NEW YEAR'S DAY.
        New York: Appleton, 1924
THE MOTHER'S RECOMPENSE. New York: Appleton, 1925
TWILIGHT SLEEP. New York: Appleton, 1927
THE CHILDREN. New York: Appleton, 1928
HUDSON RIVER BRACKETED. New York: Appleton, 1929
THE GODS ARRIVE. New York: Appleton, 1932
THE BUCCANEERS (*unfinished*). New York: Appleton-Century, 1938

ANTONIA WHITE (1899-   )

FROST IN MAY. London: Harmsworth, 1933
THE LOST TRAVELLER. London: Eyre & Spottiswoode, 1950
THE SUGAR HOUSE. London: Eyre & Spottiswoode, 1952
BEYOND THE GLASS. London: Eyre & Spottiswoode, 1954

PATRICK [VICTOR MARTINDALE] WHITE (1912-   )

HAPPY VALLEY. London: Harrap, 1939
THE LIVING AND THE DEAD. London: Routledge, 1941
THE AUNT'S STORY. London: Routledge, 1946
THE TREE OF MAN. New York: Viking, 1955. London: Eyre &
Spottiswoode, 1956
VOSS. London: Eyre & Spottiswoode, 1957. *Miles Franklin Literary
Award, 1958. W. H. Smith & Son Literary Award, 1959*
RIDERS IN THE CHARIOT. London: Eyre & Spottiswoode, 1961.
Miles Franklin Literary Award, 1962
THE SOLID MANDALA. London: Eyre & Spottiswoode, 1966

T[ERENCE] H[ANBURY] WHITE (1906-1964)

DEAD MR. NIXON (in collaboration with R. McNair Scott).
London: Cassell, 1931
THEY WINTER ABROAD (by "James Aston"). London: Chatto
& Windus, 1932
DARKNESS AT PEMBERLEY. London: Gollancz, 1932
FIRST LESSON (by "James Aston"). London: Chatto & Windus,
1932
FAREWELL VICTORIA. London: Collins, 1933
EARTH STOPPED. London: Collins, 1934
GONE TO GROUND. London: Collins, 1935
THE SWORD IN THE STONE.[1] London: Collins, 1938
THE WITCH IN THE WOOD.[1] New York: Putnam, 1939. London:
Collins, 1940
THE ILL-MADE KNIGHT.[1] New York: Putnam, 1940. London:
Collins, 1941
MISTRESS MASHAM'S REPOSE. New York: Putnam, 1946. Lon-
don: Cape, 1947
THE ELEPHANT AND THE KANGAROO. New York: Putnam,
1947. London: Cape, 1948
THE MASTER. London: Cape, 1957
THE ONCE AND FUTURE KING.[2] London: Collins, 1958

[1]Collected in THE ONCE AND FUTURE KING
[2]A tetralogy: adds THE CANDLE IN THE WIND

THORNTON [NIVEN] WILDER (1897-   )

Gold Medal for Fiction, National Institute of Arts and Letters,
1952. National Medal for Literature, 1965
THE CABALA. New York: Boni, 1926

THE BRIDGE OF SAN LUIS REY. New York: Boni, 1927. *Pulitzer Prize, 1928*
THE WOMAN OF ANDROS. New York: Boni, 1930
HEAVEN'S MY DESTINATION. London: Longmans, 1934. New York: Harper, 1935
THE IDES OF MARCH. New York: Harper, 1948

CHARLES [WALTER STANSBY] WILLIAMS (1886-1945)

WAR IN HEAVEN. London: Gollancz, 1930
MANY DIMENSIONS. London: Gollancz, 1931
THE PLACE OF THE LION. London: Mundanus, 1931
THE GREATER TRUMPS. London: Gollancz, 1932
SHADOWS OF ECSTASY. London: Gollancz, 1933
DESCENT INTO HELL. London: Faber & Faber, 1937
ALL HALLOWS' EVE. London: Faber & Faber, 1945

JOAN WILLIAMS (1928-   )

THE MORNING AND THE EVENING. New York: Atheneum, 1961
OLD POWDER MAN. New York: Harcourt, Brace & World, 1966

[THOMAS LANIER] TENNESSEE WILLIAMS (1914-   )

THE ROMAN SPRING OF MRS. STONE. New York: New Directions, 1950

WILLIAM CARLOS WILLIAMS (1883-1963)

A VOYAGE TO PAGANY. New York: Macaulay, 1928
WHITE MULE.[1] Norfolk, Conn.: New Directions, 1937
IN THE MONEY.[1] Norfolk, Conn.: New Directions, 1940
THE BUILD-UP.[1] New York: Random House, 1952
[1] A trilogy

HENRY WILLIAMSON (1897-   )

THE BEAUTIFUL YEARS.[1] London: Collins, 1921
DANDELION DAYS.[1] London: Collins, 1922
THE DREAM OF FAIR WOMEN.[1] London: Collins, 1924
THE PATHWAY.[1] London: Cape, 1928
THE PATRIOT'S PROGRESS. London: Bles, 1930
THE GOLD FALCON (Anonymous). London: Faber & Faber, 1933

THE STAR-BORN. London: Faber & Faber, 1933
THE DARK LANTERN.[2] London: Macdonald, 1951
DONKEY BOY.[2] London: Macdonald, 1952
YOUNG PHILIP MADDISON.[2] London: Macdonald, 1953
HOW DEAR IS LIFE.[2] London: Macdonald, 1954
A FOX UNDER MY CLOAK.[2] London: Macdonald, 1955
THE GOLDEN VIRGIN.[2] London: Macdonald, 1957
LOVE AND THE LOVELESS.[2] London: Macdonald, 1958
A TEST TO DESTRUCTION.[2] London: Macdonald, 1960
THE INNOCENT MOON.[2] London: Macdonald, 1961
IT WAS THE NIGHTINGALE.[2] London: Macdonald, 1962
THE POWER OF THE DEAD.[2] London: Macdonald, 1963
THE PHOENIX GENERATION.[2] London: Macdonald, 1965
A SOLITARY WAR,[2] London: Macdonald, 1966

[1]A tetralogy: THE FLAX OF DREAM, London: Faber & Faber, 1936
[2]A series: A CHRONICLE OF ANCIENT SUNLIGHT

CALDER [BAYNARD] WILLINGHAM [JR.] (1922-   )
END AS A MAN. New York: Vanguard, 1947
GERALDINE BRADSHAW. New York: Vanguard, 1950
REACH TO THE STARS. New York: Vanguard, 1951
NATURAL CHILD. New York: Dial, 1952
TO EAT A PEACH. New York: Dial, 1955
ETERNAL FIRE. New York: Vanguard, 1963

ANGUS [FRANK JOHNSTONE-] WILSON (1913-   )
HEMLOCK AND AFTER. London: Secker & Warburg, 1952
ANGLO-SAXON ATTITUDES. London: Secker & Warburg, 1956
THE MIDDLE AGE OF MRS. ELIOT. London: Secker & Warburg,
     1958. *James Tait Black Memorial Prize, 1959*
THE OLD MEN AT THE ZOO. London: Secker & Warburg, 1961
LATE CALL. London: Secker & Warburg, 1964

EDMUND WILSON (1895-   )
National Medal for Literature, 1966
I THOUGHT OF DAISY. New York: Scribner, 1929
MEMOIRS OF HECATE COUNTY. Garden City, Doubleday, 1946

ROMER WILSON, i.e. FLORENCE ROMA MUIR WILSON (1891-1930)
MARTIN SCHÜLER. London: Methuen, 1918

IF ALL THESE YOUNG MEN. London: Methuen, 1919
THE DEATH OF SOCIETY. London: Collins, 1921. *Hawthornden Prize, 1921*
THE GRAND TOUR. London: Methuen, 1923. New York: Knopf, 1923, under the title THE GRAND TOUR OF ALPHONSE MARICHAUD
DRAGON'S BLOOD. London: Collins, 1926
GREENLOW. London: Collins, 1927
LATTERDAY SYMPHONY. London: Nonesuch, 1927

DONALD WINDHAM (1920-   )
THE DOG STAR. Garden City: Doubleday, 1950
THE HERO CONTINUES. New York: Crowell, 1960
TWO PEOPLE. New York: Coward-McCann, 1965

THOMAS [CLAYTON] WOLFE (1900-1938)
LOOK HOMEWARD, ANGEL. New York: Scribner, 1929
OF TIME AND THE RIVER. New York: Scribner, 1935
THE WEB AND THE ROCK. New York: Harper, 1939
YOU CAN'T GO HOME AGAIN. New York: Harper, 1940
THE HILLS BEYOND (*fragment*). New York: Harper, 1941

H. AUSTIN WOODSLEY: See EDGAR [AUSTIN] MITTELHOLZER

[ADELINE] VIRGINIA [STEPHEN] WOOLF (1882-1941)
THE VOYAGE OUT. London: Duckworth, 1915
NIGHT AND DAY. London: Duckworth, 1919
JACOB'S ROOM. London: Hogarth, 1922
MRS. DALLOWAY. London: Hogarth, 1925.
TO THE LIGHTHOUSE. London: Hogarth, 1927. *Femina-Vie Heureuse Prize, 1928*
ORLANDO. London: Hogarth, 1928
THE WAVES. London: Hogarth, 1931
THE YEARS. London: Hogarth, 1937
BETWEEN THE ACTS. London: Hogarth, 1941

HERMAN WOUK (1915-   )
AURORA DAWN. New York: Simon & Schuster, 1947
THE CITY BOY. New York: Simon & Schuster, 1948

THE CAINE MUTINY. Garden City: Doubleday, 1951. *Pulitzer Prize, 1952*
MARJORIE MORNINGSTAR. Garden City: Doubleday, 1955
SLATTERY'S HURRICANE. New York: Permabooks, 1956
YOUNGBLOOD HAWKE. Garden City: Doubleday, 1962
DON'T STOP THE CARNIVAL. Garden City: Doubleday, 1965

RICHARD WRIGHT (1908-1960)
NATIVE SON. New York: Harper, 1940
THE OUTSIDER. New York: Harper, 1953
THE LONG DREAM. Garden City: Doubleday, 1958
LAWD TODAY. New York: Walker, 1963

ELINOR [HOYT] WYLIE (1885-1928)
JENNIFER LORN. New York: Doran, 1923
THE VENETIAN GLASS NEPHEW. New York: Doran, 1925
THE ORPHAN ANGEL. New York: Knopf, 1926. London: Heinemann, 1927, under the title MORTAL IMAGE
MR. HODGE AND MR. HAZARD. New York: Knopf, 1928

HENRY VINCENT YORKE: See HENRY GREEN

E[MILY] H[ILDA] YOUNG (1880-1949)
A CORN OF WHEAT. London: Heinemann, 1910
YONDER. London: Heinemann, 1912
MOOR FIRES. London: Murray, 1916
THE BRIDGE DIVIDING. London: Heinemann, 1922. New York: Harcourt, Brace, 1927, under the title THE MALLETTS. Reissued as THE MISSES MALLETT, London: Cape, 1927
WILLIAM. London: Cape, 1925
THE VICAR'S DAUGHTER. London: Cape, 1928
MISS MOLE. London: Cape, 1930. *James Tait Black Memorial Prize, 1931*
JENNY WREN. London: Cape, 1932
THE CURATE'S WIFE. London: Cape, 1934
CELIA. London: Cape, 1938
CHATTERTON SQUARE. London: Cape, 1947

FRANCIS BRETT YOUNG (1884-1954)
UNDERGROWTH (in collaboration with E. Brett Young). London: Secker, 1913
DEEP SEA. London: Secker, 1914

THE DARK TOWER. London: Secker, 1915
THE IRON AGE. London: Secker, 1916
THE CRESCENT MOON. London: Secker, 1918
THE YOUNG PHYSICIAN. London: Collins, 1919
THE TRAGIC BRIDE. London: Secker, 1920
THE BLACK DIAMOND. London: Collins, 1921
THE RED KNIGHT. London: Collins, 1921
PILGRIM'S REST. London: Collins, 1922
WOODSMOKE. London: Collins, 1924
COLD HARBOUR. London: Collins, 1924
SEA HORSES. London: Cassell, 1925
PORTRAIT OF CLARE. London: Heinemann, 1927. New York:
     Knopf, 1927, under the title LOVE IS ENOUGH. *James Tait
     Black Memorial Prize, 1928*
THE KEY OF LIFE. London: Heinemann, 1928
MY BROTHER JONATHAN. London: Heinemann, 1928
BLACK ROSES. London: Heinemann, 1929
JIM REDLAKE. London: Heinemann, 1930. New York: Harper,
     1930, under the title THE REDLAKES
MR. AND MRS. PENNINGTON. London: Heinemann, 1931
THE HOUSE UNDER THE WATER. London: Heinemann, 1932
THIS LITTLE WORLD. London: Heinemann, 1934
WHITE LADIES. London: Heinemann, 1935
FAR FOREST. London: Heinemann, 1936
THEY SEEK A COUNTRY. London: Heinemann, 1937
DOCTOR BRADLEY REMEMBERS. London: Heinemann, 1938
THE CITY OF GOLD. London: Heinemann, 1939
MR. LUCTON'S FREEDOM. London: Heinemann, 1940. New York:
     Reynal & Hitchcock, 1940, under the title THE HAPPY
     HIGHWAY
A MAN ABOUT THE HOUSE. London: Heinemann, 1942
WINSTANSLOW *(unfinished)*. London: Heinemann, 1956

[THOMAS] JEFFERSON YOUNG (1921-   )

A GOOD MAN. Indianapolis: Bobbs-Merrill, 1953. London: Cons-
     table, 1954, under the title A WHITE HOUSE

STARK YOUNG (1881-1963)

HEAVEN TREES. New York: Scribner, 1926
THE TORCHES FLARE. New York: Scribner, 1928
RIVER HOUSE. New York: Scribner, 1929
SO RED THE ROSE. New York: Scribner, 1934

WITHDRAWAL